Christ in
the Psalms

Christ in the Psalms

STONECROFT

HARVEST HOUSE PUBLISHERS
EUGENE, OREGON

Cover by Koechel Peterson & Associates, Inc., Minneapolis, Minnesota

Cover photo © Stockbyte / Thinkstock

CHRIST IN THE PSALMS
Stonecroft Bible Studies
Copyright © 2013 by Stonecroft Ministries, Inc.
Published by Harvest House Publishers
Eugene, Oregon 97402
www.harvesthousepublishers.com

ISBN 978-0-7369-5264-4 (pbk.)
ISBN 978-0-7369-5265-1 (eBook)

Printed in the United States of America

15 16 17 18 19 20 / VP-KBD / 10 9 8 7 6 5 4 3

Contents

Acknowledgments

Stonecroft wishes to acknowledge and thank Janice Mayo Mathers for her dedication in serving the Lord through Stonecroft. Speaker, author, and member of the Board of Directors, Jan is the primary author of revised Stonecroft Bible Studies. We appreciate her love for God's Word and her love for people who need Him. Stonecroft also thanks the team who prayed for Jan, and those who edited, designed, and offered their creative input to make these studies accessible to all.

Welcome to
Stonecroft Bible Studies!

At Stonecroft, we connect you with God, each other, and your communities.

It doesn't matter where you've been or what you've done—God wants to be in relationship with you. And one place He tells you about Himself is in His Word—the Bible. Whether the Bible is familiar or new to you, its contents will transform your life and bring answers to your biggest questions.

Gather with people in your communites—women, men, couples, young and old alike—and discover together how the psalms of the Bible point forward to the life of Jesus Christ. As you see His life in the words written hundreds of years before His birth, your confidence in the Bible will be strengthened. And you will learn about the qualities that Christ, the living God, wants to live out in your life.

Each chapter of *Christ in the Psalms* includes discussion questions to stir up meaningful conversation, specific Scripture verses to investigate, and time for prayer to connect with God and each other.

Discover more of God and His ways through this small-group exploration of the Bible.

Tips for Using This Study

This book has several features that make it easy to use and helpful for your life:

- The page number or numbers given after every Bible reference are keyed to the page numbers in the *Abundant Life Bible*. This handy paperback Bible uses the New Living Translation, a recent version in straightforward, up-to-date language. We encourage you to obtain a copy through your group leader or at stonecroft.org.

- Each chapter ends with a section called "Thoughts, Notes, and Prayer Requests." Use this space for notes or for thoughts that come to you during your group time or study, as well as prayer requests.

- In the back of the book you will find "Journal Pages"—a space available for writing down how the study is changing your life or any other personal thoughts, reactions, and reflections.

- Please make this book and study your own. We encourage you to use it and mark it in any way that helps you grow in your relationship with God!

If you find this study helpful, you may want to investigate other resources from Stonecroft. Please take a look at "Stonecroft Resources" in the back of the book or online at **stonecroft.org/store**.

stonecroft.org

Seeing Jesus Christ
in the Psalms

The entire Bible points to Christ—both the Old Testament and the New Testament. It is amazing that of all the Old Testament quotations included in the New Testament that refer to Christ, nearly one-half of them are from the psalms.

As we read through the book of Psalms, we come to many prophetic statements concerning Jesus Christ. Some psalms are entirely about Him. In others, only a verse or two refer to His life. The psalms give us the true expression of the feelings of the people who wrote them. But the sorrow, suffering, joy, and triumph find their fullest meaning in the life and on the lips of God's Son and our Savior, Jesus Christ.

In this book we have attempted to share some of the treasures found in the selected psalms that speak of Christ. You will be amazed at the accuracy of the detail and scope of these prophecies written several thousand years ago.

The study of these psalms will strengthen your faith, encourage your Christian growth, enrich your life. It will connect you more closely with the One who sacrificed Himself for us in death, was raised to new life, is seated in power at God's right hand, and will one day come to rule. The truths expressed in these ancient writings meet the needs of our lives and are as relevant today as when they were first written.

Be good to your servant,
that I may live and obey your word.
Open my eyes to see
the wonderful truths in your instructions.

—Psalm 119:17-18 (page 468)

Christlike Qualities
Psalm 1

When both of my sons received their drivers' licenses, I entered a whole new level of concern for their safety. Every time the phone rang when they were gone, I knew it was bad news. Not until the car pulled into the garage could I finally relax. During this time, I maintained my sanity through Scripture memorization—filling my head with the protection of God's Word.

I had been memorizing Psalm 112, and one morning verse 7 kept looping through my mind. *"They do not fear bad news; they confidently trust the LORD to care for them"* (Psalm 112:7, page 466). All morning long that phrase played over in my mind. *"They do not fear bad news... they do not fear bad news..."*

That afternoon, about the time the boys were due home from school, the phone rang. It was the call I'd lived in fear of—my youngest son had been in an accident and was being taken to the hospital. As I rushed to the car and drove to the hospital, an unbelievable peace saturated every pore of my being—an uncanny calm. I knew I should be shaken to my core, but God, through memorized Scripture, had spent the morning reminding me I didn't have to fear bad news. Thankfully, my son's injuries were minor, but I had that overpowering peace before I knew the outcome.

Scripture memorization is a great gift you can give yourself. The book we're focusing on in this study is filled with passages that, if committed to memory, will greatly enrich your life.

❦

Prayer

Lord, how sweet your words taste to me; they are sweeter than honey. Your commandments give me understanding. Thank you for your wonderful Word that is always a lamp to guide my feet and a light for my path (Psalm 119:103-105, page 470).

The book of Psalms is far more than a collection of poetry. It is also a book of ancient Jewish history that gives us a glimpse into the culture, philosophy, faith, and even politics of that time—all artfully woven into poetry, songs, and prayers. This book appeals to the heart more than any other book of the Bible. It's as if the Spirit of God gathered into these 150 poems all the emotions and experiences of life—love and rejection, triumph and tragedy, hope and despair, redemption and deceit. It is all there for our inspiration and instruction.

Originally, Psalms was the national songbook for the Jewish nation. The actual meaning of the word *psalm* involves the idea of instrumental accompaniment. The Hebrew title of the book means *Book of Praises*. Its purpose is summed up in Psalm 95:1-2 (page 457):

Come, let us sing to the LORD!
Let us shout joyfully to the Rock of our salvation.
Let us come to him with thanksgiving.
Let us sing psalms of praise to him.

Psalms is divided into five sections—each section corresponding to one of the first five books of the Bible.

- Section 1, Psalms 1–41, corresponds with Genesis and is about the beginning of humankind and God's plan for us.

- Section 2, Psalms 42–72, corresponds with Exodus and is about God's deliverance of the Israelites.

- Section 3, Psalms 73–89, corresponds with Leviticus and is about the worship of God in His sanctuary.

- Section 4, Psalms 90–106, corresponds with Numbers and is about the peril and protection of God's people.

- Section 5, Psalms 107–150, corresponds with Deuteronomy and is about how God overrules all trials, difficulties, and perplexities. It is also about praise and worship.

This book has been beloved by Christians all around the world, throughout the centuries—they've incorporated it into their worship, their singing, and their praying. For many early churches it was their only songbook. Later, some monasteries even assigned specific psalms to be read at certain hours of each day so that the whole book was read in the course of a week.

Psalms is quoted in the New Testament more often than any other Old Testament book. There are 70 to 93 quotations, depending on if you count only verbatim quotes or all references. The psalms are timeless, applicable to every place we find ourselves, reflecting the full range of experiences and feelings we encounter in life. More importantly, the book of Psalms is full of Christ: His humanity, His sacrifice, His rejection, His exaltation, and His victory. Every aspect of Christ is there.

And think of this! Jesus knew and loved the psalms. He quoted from them many times while He was on earth.

Perhaps for some, this is your first time to really explore the book of Psalms. For others, maybe you have long drawn comfort and encouragement from this ancient book. Regardless, this journey together will be a time of wonderful fellowship, as we discover what the psalms teach us about Christ.

Psalm 1: Christlike Qualities

While Psalm 1 is not widely viewed as a psalm about Christ, its contents and character certainly speak to the attributes of Jesus. Some of the ancient interpreters believed that this psalm was intended to describe the character and reward of the Lord Jesus.* So, let's get started.

The Great Contrast

This psalm is an inspired preface because it frames the theme of the entire book. It answers many questions, such as, how can a person be joyful? How important is the kind of company we keep? What is worthwhile in life? What is going to last in life?

It begins by contrasting two types of people: the godly and the wicked. Jesus made similar comparisons in His teaching when He contrasted sheep and goats, wise and foolish bridesmaids, or the narrow and broad gateways. Psalm 1 is only six verses, so let's read all of it (page 415).

On the chart below note the contrast between the characteristics of the godly and the wicked, evil, or ungodly.

Psalm 1 Contrasts

Psalm 1 verse	The Godly:	TheWicked/Evil/Ungodly:
Verse 1		
Verse 2		
Verse 3		
Verse 4		
Verse 5		
Verse 6		

---

* Charles Spurgeon, in *The Treasury of David,* his great book on the Psalms, quotes John Fry as stating this.

It draws a very stark contrast, doesn't it? Which contrasting characteristic struck you personally?

The psalm begins with a shout, *"Oh, the joys of those who do not follow the advice of the wicked, or stand around with sinners, or join in with mockers."* Do you know what the author is talking about? He's talking about the person who follows God's plan. That person knows what true joy is!

Later on, in Psalm 32:1 (page 427), it tells us even more explicitly who is joyful. *"Oh, what joy for those whose disobedience is forgiven!"* Joy is the result of knowing that God no longer counts our sin against us. When we recognize Jesus as our Savior—our life does a complete 180. We exchange one way of life for one that is immensely more satisfying. It's like starting out on a brand-new page, without a single mark on it—and, in the process, we begin to experience a whole new level of joy.

In Psalm 1:1 we see the downward cycle of a life that excludes God. First, you listen to the advice of others who don't acknowledge God. Then you begin to follow their example. Finally, you find yourself right in the middle of them, mocking the truth that God planted in your heart.

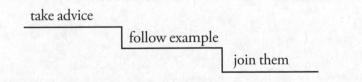

take advice
     follow example
          join them

Read Romans 1:19-20 (page 857).

According to these verses, how should people know there is a God?

God created us to know Him and to be in relationship with Him. Our lives truly work only in conjunction with Him. In fact, it is impossible to reach our full potential outside of Him. And the further we distance ourselves from Him, the less meaningful our lives become; it is an inescapable downward cycle!

Why do people have no excuse for *not* knowing God?

Refusing to acknowledge God, to live the life He designed for us, is sin and the Bible tells us that we are all sinners. Read Romans 3:23 (on page 859).

Now read Romans 6:23 (page 861).

What is the free *"gift of God,"* and who is it through?

Yes! Eternal life. We have an option! Death or life—downward cycle or upward cycle. That eternal life is offered through Jesus Christ our Lord.

God sent His only Son, Jesus Christ, to pay the price for our sins, because He loves us and desires for us to be in relationship with Him. Did you notice it referred to what Jesus did as a *"free gift"*? Until we accept that gift, by recognizing that Jesus died for us, we will be held accountable for our sins and not experience true life. We will remain in a downward cycle, in a state of spiritual death, which will eventually lead to eternal separation from God. Without a relationship with Him, the advice of the wicked, which is to continue to ignore Him, will have greater appeal to us and will result in greater limitations on our lives.

According to Psalm 16:7-8 (pages 419-420), who should we take advice from?

Jesus guides those who have accepted Him as their Savior. And as He guides us, our lives are transformed.

Delighting In God and His Word

Verse 1 describes what a godly person does not do. List the two actions verse 2 says a godly person *does* do.

1.

2.

What are some things you delight in?

Why do you delight in these things?

This is the point: When you delight in something or someone, you look for opportunities to expose yourself to the object of your delight. If you want to delight in God's Word, look for opportunities to expose yourself to it. The more you read it, the more delightful and vital it will become to you.

The second thing a godly person does is meditate on God's Word. Meditation is like chewing. When you chew food, it extracts the flavor and distributes it over all your taste buds. It also extracts the nutrition and enables your body to fully utilize it. That's what meditation does. It fills your mind with the flavor of God's Word and sends its truth and wisdom into your mind and spirit so you can fully benefit from it.

As you read your Bible, when a verse or passage raises a question, sparks a thought, or impacts you in some way, mull over it throughout the day. Keep your Bible handy so you can go back to it, or write it on a piece of paper or input it into your smartphone. The more you meditate on God's Word, the more value you will extract from it. The more value you extract, the more it will delight you. It becomes an exciting cycle of ever-increasing growth that positively influences your thoughts and behaviors.

One of the best tools for meditation is memorization. As you work to commit a passage to memory, you are filling your mind with those words, and you will find they come to life for you. If you've never tried memorizing Scripture, Psalm 1 is an excellent place to start. Copy the verses onto 3x5 cards that you can keep with you. Work on one verse at a time until the psalm is memorized. You won't believe how wonderful you feel when it is all memorized! A side benefit to Scripture memorization, according to medical science, is that it's good exercise for maintaining brain health.

Read Psalm 1:3.

There is another passage in Psalms that uses the analogy of a tree. Read Psalm 92:12-14 (page 456).

What adjectives does the psalmist use to describe the godly in this passage?

Oh, this is such an incredible analogy, isn't it? A Christian is like a tree which has been transplanted, not a wild tree but a purposefully placed tree, exactly where God wants us—into His presence! We do not have to fear getting older.

Finally, what do the trees in Psalm 1:3 do?

When we are planted in God, our life will glorify God, which is the definition of success. Even during a time of personal drought, He will provide us with the living water needed to consistently glorify Him. It is impossible to wither when we stay connected to God. He alone produces life!

Read Psalm 1:4.

What a deplorable contrast—*chaff*—or in other words, the throwaway part of a seed or grain! It has no life and no fruit; it perishes and leaves nothing behind. For a little while it was associated with the plant on which it grew and enjoyed its benefits, but the time of separation inevitably came. Read Psalm 1:5-6.

Read 1 John 5:11-12 (page 943). How is this passage related to Psalm 1:5-6?

Choosing Life

The important thing to remember is that we have a choice. God placed within us at creation a free will. He gives people equal opportunity to choose life over death, but He longs for us to choose life. Read 2 Peter 3:9 (page 939).

What is God's desire?

God will not force us to choose life. He leaves it up to us. What have you chosen? (For more information, see "Know God" on pages 177–179.)

Based on Psalm 1, what would you say is the secret of true joy?

We've been talking about the Psalm 1 description of a godly person. Truly, this passage speaks of the qualities and attributes of Jesus Christ. He is the only truly righteous Man, and it is only through Christ that we are able to have a relationship with God.

Since this psalm talks about the importance of meditation, let's close this chapter by giving it a try. Picture in your mind everything this passage mentions about the godly: a riverbank and a healthy tree with leaves unfurled, fruit hanging from its branches. Imagine the sap running through the trunk and branches, nurturing them internally. Imagine the warmth of the sun and fresh air nurturing the tree externally. Imagine the sound of the river, the smell of the soil, the feel of the bark and leaves, and, of course, the sweet taste of the fruit. Focus on that picture for several moments until it comes to life in your mind and then describe or sketch it below.

Can you imagine yourself in place of the tree, as described in the verses we just read? What might that be like, to stand strong and healthy beside God's River of Life? Feel God's wisdom and guidance surging through you. Feel His Spirit warming you with His unlimited potential. Smell the fragrance of His creativity filling your mind, and feel the weight of the fruit you are bearing for Him. Taste the satisfaction of His pleasure in you. Keep concentrating on this picture until it is as real as the other picture you imagined, and then describe or sketch what you saw.

Thank God for the picture He gave you. Keep it in your mind. Examine it at night before you go to sleep and fix it in your mind again when you wake up. Choose to be the godly person Psalm 1 describes.

—————— *Personal Reflection and Application* ——————

From this chapter,

I see…

I believe…

I will…

Prayer

God, I want to start hiding your Word in my heart that I might not sin against you. Teach me what is true, and make me realize what is wrong in my life. Correct me when I am wrong, and teach me to do what is right (Psalm 119:11, page 468, and 2 Timothy 3:16, page 915).

Thoughts, Notes, and Prayer Requests

_____

_____

_____

_____

_____

_____

_____

_____

_____

_____

_____

_____

_____

_____

_____

_____

_____

_____

Christ—The Messiah
Psalm 2
Christ—The King of Kings
Psalm 72

J esus Christ came to earth as a baby. He willingly took on human limitations, experienced human temptation and emotion, and yet remained without sin. His death and resurrection paved the way for us to be reconciled with God, our Creator. The Bible tells us that Jesus will return to earth a second time, but this time it will be without any limitations whatsoever. He will return in the full power of God and establish His kingdom here on earth.

❦

Prayer

Father, I know that Jesus is your dearly loved Son (and that He brings you great joy). I look forward to the day when every knee will bend before Him—the King of kings—and every tongue will confess and give praise to you (Matthew 3:17, page 735, and Romans 14:11, page 867).

Psalm 2: Christ—The Messiah

When Jesus came to earth, people failed to recognize Him as the promised Messiah because they were expecting Him to arrive with all the pomp and circumstance of a king. Instead, He arrived in an obscure manger as a helpless baby, the antithesis of their expectation. In Psalm 2, God presents His Son, Jesus Christ, as Ruler over all things.

God's Plan to Exalt His Son

Historically, this psalm is about King David being established on his throne in spite of opposition from his enemies. Prophetically, however, it speaks of God's plan to exalt His Son, Jesus Christ, and have Him reign over all His enemies.

This psalm is full of action. Crowds are raging! People are rioting! Kings are rallying their forces, and summits are being called! Woven through the action is God's amusement at the puny plans of humanity as He announces Christ as the coming King who will rule over all the earth.

There are four voices speaking in Psalm 2:

- In Psalm 2:1-3 we hear the voice of the ungodly people of the world.

- In Psalm 2:4-6 we hear the voice of God.

- In Psalm 2:7-9 we hear the voice of God's Son, the rejected Messiah.

- In Psalm 2:10-12 we hear the advice being given to kings and all in authority to obey and worship the Lord.

Altogether, parts of this psalm are quoted ten times in the New Testament, as we'll soon see. Let's begin with the first section of the psalm. Read Psalm 2:1-3 (page 415).

These verses are quoted almost verbatim in a prayer the early Christians prayed after Jesus had been crucified. Read Acts 4:25-28 (page 833).

What do verses 27 and 28 say about this psalm? How do you think they responded when they realized that they were in the city where the prophetic words of Psalm 2, spoken hundreds of years before, had recently been lived out?

How would you have reacted?

Read Psalm 2:1 again. How are the nations' plans described?

rebellious
plotting

These early Christians are firsthand witnesses to the futility of human plans that are made in opposition to God. They have personal knowledge of the resurrection of Jesus! And isn't it the same for us? Does it fill you with even greater confidence in God, reading the fulfillment of these ancient words, knowing all that has come to pass since that time? Nations, organizations, and people are always going to be rising up against God, *but we do not have to fear them*—because we have personal knowledge of the power of God to defeat those plans!

In Psalm 2:4-6 the scene changes to heaven, and it is God's voice we hear.

In verse 4, what is God's reaction to the plans being made against Him?

What does God do in verse 5?

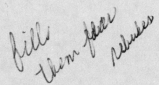

Do you think God is being unreasonable? Why or why not?

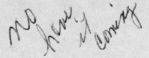

There is no way we can truly comprehend all of God's ways because His mind is so far beyond ours. But even with our limited ability, imagine what it looks like from His perspective. From the beginning of creation, His plan for us has been based in an unfathomable love. He wanted to pour His love over us and enrich our lives with a close relationship with Him. In that love, He gave us the privilege of free will. But right from the start, our free will has manifested itself in an independent nature that flaunts our determination to live separately from Him.

Submitting to the Son

This is the beautiful part of what God is saying in this psalm. People thought they had thwarted His plans when they killed His Son. But overcoming death was nothing for Him. When Jesus was resurrected three days later, death forever lost its power. God's plan is still unfolding, and although people will continue to plot against Him, they will not succeed. Jesus is returning and He will be King over all—just as He promised in Psalm 2:6. And, as always, it's our choice whose side we will be on.

In Psalm 2:7-9 we hear Jesus Christ repeating what God has told Him—that He is the chosen King. The apostle Paul quoted verse 7 while speaking to people in Antioch. Read Acts 13:32-34 (page 842).

What section of Psalm 2 did Paul quote to show that its fulfillment was in Jesus?

The phrase *"become your Father"* (Acts 13:33 and Psalm 2:7) is not the only time God referred to Jesus as His Son. Several times when Jesus was on earth, God spoke from heaven saying the same thing. Read the following verses.

Matthew 3:17 (page 735)

Matthew 17:5 (page 748)

2 Peter 1:17-18 (page 938)

What is the common characteristic in all three of these passages?

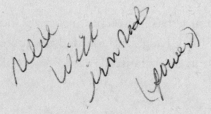

Now read Psalm 2:8-9 (page 415).

What do you think God is saying to Jesus in these verses?

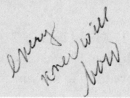

For now, all humanity still has a choice in whether or not they will recognize Jesus as God's Son. That will not always be the case. Read Romans 14:11 (page 867).

In the end, what will everyone do?

Psalm 2:10-12 lists five directives and gives both a warning and a promise. As you read this passage, list the five directives given.

1.

2. _Wise_

3. _Warned_

4. _serve the Lord_

5. _truth_

"*Submit to God's royal son*" means to make peace with God, embrace His Son, obey Him, and depend on Him as our Sovereign King.

What is the warning?

(Perish)   _to be loyal_   _Kiss his feet_

God is first and foremost infinitely loving, but He does not take lightly the rejection of His Son who paid such a terrible price for us. His anger is righteous and justified. Now read Psalm 30:5a (page 426).

What will come once His anger has subsided?

God is quick, even eager, to forgive us when we turn back to Him. He is waiting to shower us with His favor—which brings us to the promise at the end of Psalm 2:12.

What will you receive when you take refuge in Him?

Joy and refuge! In Christ we have a refuge that cannot be breached and in that refuge we find joy!

What is the significance of joy resulting from taking refuge in Christ?

Psalm 72: Christ—The King of Kings

In Psalm 2, God announces His Son, Jesus Christ, as the coming King. In Psalm 72 (pages 445-446) we read the very moving prayer King David prayed for his son, Solomon, as he took over the throne of Israel. David's prayer for his son, however, is also a prophecy of the coming reign of the King of kings—Jesus Christ. God gave David certain promises concerning the glory of Solomon's kingdom that are also promises concerning Jesus, who will rule forever.

As you read this psalm, remember it is a father praying for his son. David, who personally knows the heavy weight and responsibility of kingship that his son will carry, is asking God to bless every aspect of his rule. It is a very moving prayer. Remember too, it is describing the Kingdom of God that is to come.

How is the Kingdom described in the following verses?

Psalm 72:1-2

righteness — justice fair

Psalm 72:3

prosperity

Psalm 72:4

defend the cause of needy

Psalm 72:6-8

rain richness flourish

Psalm 72:9 *bow down*

Psalm 72:12-14

look after the oppressed

Psalm 72:16

supply plenty (good times)

As moving as it is to read this father's prayer for his son's rule, it is even more moving to read it in light of Jesus Christ's reign on earth. The first four verses describe the righteousness and justice of Jesus' eventual reign, which was introduced in Psalm 2. The result is peace and prosperity for all.

According to Psalm 72:5-7, what is the length of Jesus' reign?

forever

Empires come and go, but the Kingdom of our God will stand forever.

According to Psalm 72:8-11, how far will His Kingdom extend?

from sea to sea

Two other verses that speak to this are Psalm 86:9 (page 453) and Psalm 138:4 (page 476).

> How do these other psalm passages add to how the Kingdom is described in Psalm 72?

The Beauty of God's Kingdom

Up to this point, the psalm has stressed the King's reign and authority over all nations. The next part shows His gentle helpfulness. Read Psalm 72:12-14 (page 445).

> How do these verses reflect God's compassion?
>
> *help needy save from death*

> Why will Jesus redeem the oppressed?
>
> *precious in his sight*

Our lives are precious to Christ! He is our rescuer and defender. How wonderful!

Verses 16-17 tell us about the abundance and happiness we will experience in this Kingdom. Don't you love the picture of well-being this paints? I love the phrase about thriving like grass. Oh, the wonder of the Kingdom that Jesus will reign over one day! He was rejected the first time, but not this time. As we've already read, everyone will recognize Him as King and will worship Him.

If you noticed, scattered throughout this psalm are descriptions of how the people will respond to Jesus when He returns. Read the following passages. How did the people respond in each verse?

Psalm 72:5

Psalm 72:9

Psalm 72:10

Psalm 72:11

Psalm 72:15

Psalm 72:17

more & more things
all generations   *Bless him*

What kind of picture do these verses paint about the Kingdom of God?

Wounderful
bow down
for ever

David concludes his prayer for his son by worshipping the ultimate King who rules over the entire world. Read verses Psalm 72:18-20 (page 446).

When David signs his name at the very end, you can almost see him hand the crown over to his son. He doesn't sign his name with the royal title of king—rather just David, son of Jesse.

What are some reasons he might have done this?

humble

In Psalm 2 we see Christ, our Savior—the Messiah everyone rejected. In Psalm 72 we see Christ, the coming King, whom no one will reject. In both psalms, we see the enduring love of God, our heavenly Father. Take a few moments and thank God for the gift of His Son, who is both our Messiah and King.

——————— *Personal Reflection and Application* ———————

From this chapter,

I see...

I believe...

I will...

———————————— ❧ ————————————

Prayer

God, thank you for saving me, not because of the righteous things I have done, but because of your mercy. You washed away my sins, giving me a new birth and new life through the Holy Spirit. I testify that you sent your Son to be the Savior of the world (Titus 3:5-6, page 918, and 1 John 4:14, page 943).

——————— *Thoughts, Notes, and Prayer Requests* ———————

_____

_____

_____

_____

_____

3

Christ—The Sovereign Creator
Psalm 8

We'd just gone through perhaps the most extraordinary few days of our lives. A 24-hour plane ride had delivered us to La Paz, Bolivia, a city that sits nearly 12,000 feet above sea level, high in the Andes Mountains. It is a city steeped in poverty—poverty that overwhelmed us as we walked the streets, straining for breath in the thin air.

A couple of days later we boarded a bus for a ten-hour heart-stopping journey that sent us careening down the mountainside toward the jungle, on a road so narrow and winding that the bus kept scraping the side of the slope. The scenery was spectacular, though somewhat diminished by our concern for our lives. In Cochabamba we were met by two men who squeezed us into an open jeep already filled with two weeks' worth of supplies, and off we roared for another six bone-jarring hours into endless barren mountain country that gave new meaning to desolate.

We had come so my husband could drill a well in a village suffering from years of drought. In America it had all sounded like an adventure. By the time we climbed out of the jeep in the tiny village of Mizque, it felt close to a nightmare. The sun was just setting as we arrived and we quickly unloaded, washed the top layer of dirt off our skin, and ate a hastily prepared meal. Darkness fell quickly, and we decided to go outside for some fresh air before climbing into bed.

The sight awaiting us literally took our breath away. The four of us stood in absolute silence as we stared up at the night sky. There on the high barren plain nothing obstructed our view. There were no street lights for hundreds of miles—no lights at all. All we could see for as far as our eyes could reach was the magnificent nighttime sky. It wrapped around us like warm, diamond-studded velvet. The stars weren't above us, they were around us—so close that I actually reached my hand out as if I could touch them.

The presence of God was just as close, brilliant in the midst of His magnificent creation. It was a dimension of His presence I'd never before experienced. I thought of the words in Psalms: *"When I look at the night sky and see the work of your fingers—the moon and the stars you set in place—what are people that you should think about them, mere mortals that you should care for them?"* (Psalm 8:3-4, page 417).

And yet He did think of and care for us—so much that He sent His Son to die for us. Oh Lord, you are worthy of all praise!

Prayer

God, you are the Creator! The heavens proclaim your glory and the skies display your craftsmanship day after day and night after night. Your creation makes you known throughout the earth to all the world (Psalm 19:1-4, page 421).

A great way to start your day is by reading a psalm. Some people make a practice of reading five psalms each day. Since there are 150 psalms, by following this pattern, you can read the whole book of Psalms each month. Or, you may read two psalms a day, one in the morning and one at night. If you do that, you will have read the whole book of Psalms in less than three months.

In Psalm 2 we saw Christ as the Messiah, and in Psalm 72 we saw Christ as the King of kings. Now we're going to look at Psalm 8 (page 417), a beautiful psalm that shows Christ as the Sovereign Creator.

God, the All-Powerful Creator

In addition to Psalm 8, there are several others that praise the mighty power of God in creating the universe:

- Psalm 19 speaks of His creating the sun

- Psalm 104 speaks of His orchestrating various aspects of creation

- Psalm 29 speaks of His making storms and earthquakes

- These psalms use the world of nature to show us that God's presence fills the earth. Nature is full of God, show-casing His glory everywhere we look. Let's begin by look-ing at some verses in the New Testament. Read the following passages and note everything they say about creation.

John 1:1-5 (page 809)

Hebrews 1:2-3 (page 920)

Colossians 1:15-16 (page 902)

According to these verses, how was the earth created?

Jesus

Did you notice in Colossians 1:16 that God created even the things we cannot see?

What are the examples of the things He created that we cannot see?

It forms a picture of the sovereignty of God, doesn't it? Even the ruling powers on this earth are put in place by Him!

Which phrase in these verses did you find most significant?

The verse that struck me is John 1:5: *"The light shines in the darkness, and the darkness can never extinguish it."* This verse paints a very clear picture of God's sovereignty. God's light penetrates the deepest darkness. Combine all the darkness in the world—and there's a lot of it—throw in the darkness of Satan's realm, and it still cannot even come close to extinguishing the light of God. The light of His sovereign power and authority and love will always overcome the darkness.

That is praiseworthy stuff, don't you think? Let's stop for a moment and acknowledge God's light, which shines through every dark circumstance of our lives. Write down the dark circumstances facing you right now and then hold them out to God. Ask Him to let His healing light penetrate these situations. Also ask Him to reveal your part in the darkness—an attitude or behavior—that might be preventing His light from shining through you.

A Revelation of God's Character

Now let's read Psalm 8 (page 417).

How does creation reveal the majesty and glory of God?

What is the statement this psalm begins and ends with?

Did you notice that both times, the first *Lord* is written in capital letters—

I am" or "I will be who I will be." This name emphasizes His self-existence. When *Lord* is written with small letters, it translates the Hebrew word *Adonai*, which means Master or Lord. It emphasizes God's role as Ruler of the earth. (The word *adonai* can also refer to people, and in this case it also means "master," "ruler," or "lord.")

God is referred to in many different ways throughout the Bible, each reference giving us a fuller picture of His deity. Read the following Scriptures and note how they refer to God.

Genesis 16:13 (page 13)

Genesis 17:1 (page 13)

Genesis 22:14 (page 17)

Exodus 3:14 (page 45)

Judges 6:24 (page 193)

Psalm 9:2 (page 417)

Psalm 84:1 (page 452)

almighty

Which name has the most significance in your life? Please explain. *wonderful mighty, Prince of peace*

Jesus is also referred to in many different ways. Read the following verses for some examples and note what they say.

Isaiah 9:6 (page 523)

type Prince

Hebrews 4:14 (page 922)

John 1:29 (page 809) *Lamb of God*

Acts 10:36 (page 839)

Lord of all

John 11:25 (page 820)

I am the resurrection

Which names do you most often use to refer to Jesus? How do these names reflect your belief of who He is?

The Creator Who Knows Us *next time*

The first two verses of Psalm 8 portray sweeping expanses and huge contrasts. They tell us that God's splendor is not only seen here on earth but also far beyond the heavens, which can't even be seen—further than we can even comprehend. It uses the innocence of infants and the evil of enemies to illustrate His mighty strength.

As we read in the first chapter, creation so thoroughly provides evidence of God that there is no excuse for doubting His existence. (Romans 1:20, page 857). His glory is so conspicuous that even small children see and acknowledge it. In fact, Jesus referred to Psalm 8:2 when some religious leaders were indignant that children were worshipping Him. Read Matthew 21:15-16 (page 751).

The contrast drawn between infants and enemies is an excellent example of how God uses unexpected means to demonstrate His power.

What does 1 Corinthians 1:26-28 (page 870) have to add to this discussion?

No one expected the redeeming power of God to arrive in the form of an infant, and yet that infant, when He returns as King, will silence all enemies forever.

Read Psalm 8:3-4 (page 417).

Every time I look up at the night sky, just as I did in the village of Mizque, these verses come to mind. What thoughts or emotions do they evoke?

Does the reference to God's fingers stir up a whirlwind of imagery? Can you see Him contemplating where to place each star, moving them around the sky with His fingers until they are displayed to perfection? Can you see Him lining up the three stars that form the belt of the constellation Orion, smiling to Himself as He looks ahead to when stargazers will decide that particular grouping of stars resembles a hunter?

While verse 3 inspires delightful imagery, verse 4 inspires immense awe. What question does it ask?

Does it amaze you to think about Almighty God, Creator of the universe, thinking about *you*? But He does—all the time! Psalm 139 describes in exquisite detail just how aware and involved God is with our lives. Nothing about us escapes His loving attention. Notice what Psalm 139:17-18 (page 476) says about God's thoughts about us.

Did you catch that? *"They outnumber the grains of sand!"* Isn't that incredible to think about? We are never out of God's mind!

Read Matthew 10:30-31 (page 741). How does it compare people to sparrows?

Descriptions of God's loving care are woven throughout the entire Bible. A few are listed below. How is God's love manifested in each passage?

Romans 5:8 (page 860)

Psalm 136:26 (page 475)

Ephesians 3:18-19 (page 896)

When we meditate on the greatness of God, who made the endless universe, and we realize that He is concerned about every detail in our lives, it is impossible *not* to be awestruck, isn't it? God wants to have a relationship with the people He created!

Read Psalm 8:5 (page 417).

What are we crowned with?

When we acknowledge the price Jesus paid for our sins, then we are elevated to a position of joint heir with Jesus in God's Kingdom. Read Ephesians 3:6 (page 896).

Both Gentiles and Jews will share in the blessings and inheritance as God's children. This is possible only because on the cross, Jesus became the intermediary between God and us. Read Hebrews 7:25 (pages 923-924).

Because of Jesus, God does not see us as sinful. He sees us as good! Now read 2 Corinthians 5:21 (page 884).

Describe the exchange you read about:

Jesus took our sins

Inconceivable! And yet true—because Jesus loves us.
Read Psalm 8:6-8.

People were created by God and given a position of authority and responsibility! What exactly has God put us in charge of,
according to verse 6?

to be controlled by the spirit

Loss and Restoration

In the Garden of Eden, humans had full dominion over all creatures. This was God's plan. In the first book of the Bible, Genesis 1:26-
28 (page 3) says,

> *"Then God said, 'Let us make human beings in our image, to be like us.*
> *They will reign over the fish in the sea, the birds in the sky,*
> *the livestock, all the wild animals on the earth,*
> *and the small animals that scurry along the ground.'*
> *So God created human beings in his own image.*
> *In the image of God he created them; male and female he created them.*
> *Then God blessed them and said, 'Be fruitful and multiply.*
> *Fill the earth and govern it. Reign over the fish in the sea,*
> *the birds in the sky, and all the animals that scurry along the ground.'"*

However, when people chose to follow Satan rather than God, Satan gained an advantage over them, and God's beautiful creation changed drastically. The relationship between God and people changed and the relationship between all living creatures changed.

Read Romans 8:20-23 (page 862) and note the points you find important.

This broken relationship can be restored only in Christ. What this passage is talking about is that, when Jesus returns to earth to establish His Kingdom, the relationship between Creator and creation will be restored.

What will this Kingdom look like, according to Isaiah 11:6-9 (page 526)?

It's a beautiful picture of incredible peace and fellowship between all of God's creation—just as He originally planned.

And now we come to the last verse—a repeat of the first verse: *"Oh LORD, our Lord, your majestic name fills the earth!"* Reflect on your thoughts regarding the psalms you've studied so far. In response, write your own brief psalm of worship.

─────── *Personal Reflection and Application* ───────

From this chapter,

I see…

I believe…

I will…

───────────── ∞ ─────────────

Prayer

    Lord, I will not let my heart be troubled. I have put my trust in you and know that you are preparing a place for me right now. I know that when everything is ready, you will come and get me, so that I will always be with you. I look forward to the prize that awaits me—the crown of righteousness, which you, the righteous Judge, will give me on the day of your return (John 14:1-3, page 823, and 2 Timothy 4:8, pages 915-916).

─────── *Thoughts, Notes, and Prayer Requests* ───────

_____

_____

_____

_____

_____

4

The Resurrected Christ
Psalm 16

It was the day before my ninth Easter and I was feeling very sorry for myself. My father had died the year before, and it was like our family had been dumped in a food processor and whirred on high. Everything was mixed up, the texture of our life unrecognizable. Now it was almost Easter and, for the first time ever, I didn't have a new dress to wear to church. It was a symbol of all that had changed in our life. To make a bleak picture even bleaker, my best friend called to tell me about the new dress her daddy had just bought her. I went to bed hoping Easter would never arrive.

The next morning I moped my way into the kitchen and there, sitting on the kitchen counter, was a brand-new pair of shoes. Oh! They were such beautiful shoes—green, my favorite color. I looked at my mom in wonder, but she just smiled and shrugged. "They were here when I got up," she said. "I guess the Easter Bunny brought them." I was old enough to know they didn't come from the Easter Bunny, and although I didn't know how Mom had managed it, I was thrilled. I didn't know anyone lucky enough to have green shoes.

As it turned out, Mom had created them by mixing green food coloring into some white shoe polish and coating an old pair of my shoes. Unfortunately, it had snowed that night and my shoe polish wasn't waterproof. I left little green footprints all the way to church.

But I didn't mind, because I've never felt as pretty as I did that Easter morning in those green shoes. Love makes you feel beautiful and I knew I was loved.

It wasn't long afterward that I discovered the real meaning to Easter. It had nothing to do with the Easter Bunny, a new dress, or even my green shoes. Easter was about a *father*—my heavenly Father, who loved me so much He sent His Son, Jesus, to die for my sins. But even more remarkable is the fact that three days later Jesus came back to life. His resurrection made it possible for me to have a relationship with my heavenly Father that not even death could destroy.

∞

Prayer

Thank you, Father, for loving me so much that you gave your one and only Son so that if I believe in Him, I will not perish but have eternal life. Thank you too for sending your Son to this world, not to judge the world, but to save the world (John 3:16-17, page 811).

Rejoicing in God's Protection

Psalm 16 (pages 419-420) is a bright song of joy that comes from the trusting, faithful heart of David. Some of the psalms have a designation that describes the character of the poem, and the designation of this one is "miktam of David." *Miktam* is probably a literary or musical term. It is a prayerful meditation on the prophecies of Jesus' death and resurrection. First, read through the whole psalm to get a feel for it. Afterward, we'll come back for a closer look.

David's love and gratitude for God are obvious as you read this psalm, aren't they? It's clear his relationship with God is a significant influence in his life.

What does David ask for in the first verse?

Psalm 16:1 is the prayer of one who knows what it means to take refuge in the Lord. As a king who frequently went to war, David knew how vital a place of refuge was. He had also experienced firsthand that God is the only refuge that is 100 percent secure. The Hebrew word for God that David called on in this verse means "the Strong One, the Mighty God, the Omnipotent Helper of His people." Isn't that exactly who you'd want to run to when in need of refuge?

There are many other verses in the Bible that tell us about the protection God gives to those who trust in Him. Read the following verses and note all of God's promises.

Psalm 31:19 (page 427)

Psalm 34:7-8 (page 428)

Psalm 37:3-5 (page 429)

Psalm 118:8 (page 468)

2 Timothy 4:18 (page 916)

Now look back over this incredible list. What is the underlying theme of these verses?

The very first verse was my favorite. To think that God *stores up* goodness to lavish on us when we come to Him for protection. Just think about that. What shape do you tend to be in emotionally when you need protection from something?

If ever someone needs goodness poured over them, it is when they are seeking refuge and safety. In her book *Infidel,* Ayaan Hirsi Ali tells about rescuing members of her family from a refugee camp. They had fled for their lives during the horror of Somalia's collapse and were now destitute and starved—some on the verge of death. Ali managed to get 20 family members through the barricades by giving gigantic bribes to the guards. She described the incredible joy and relief it was to finally reach her mother's house, where waiting relatives took in the refugees, lavishing upon them food, water, medical care, and most important of all—safety.* In much greater proportions, this is the refuge we have in God.

Making Choices

Are you beginning to see the value in meditating on Scripture every day—especially the psalms? How differently do you think your day might go if every morning you read over verses such as the ones we just read? God's Word empowers you to face the daily circumstances of life like nothing else in this world can!

Read Psalm 16:2. How does David refer to God? What does that tell you about his relationship with God?

We are not automatically Christians because of the family we are born into or because we were brought up in church. Each person must make a conscious choice to put their trust in God. Psalm 63 (page 441) shows how David chose to completely align himself with God.

Read verses 1-8 and note the phrases that describe how he feels about God.

---

* Ayaan Hirsi Ali, *Infidel*, (New York: Free Press, 2007), pages 148-149, 159-160.

How does your commitment compare to David's commitment to God?

David openly expressed his love for God. He earnestly sought Him out because having a strong relationship with Him satisfied his innermost longings. David recognized God's unfailing love for him and how much He had helped him. In response, David praised God and sang for joy. We can learn from David that worship should be a natural response to our encounters with God.

Going back to Psalm 16, who does David call his heroes in verse 3?

What is the irony of King David calling the godly people in the land his heroes?

How is verse 4 different from verse 3?

In David's day, there was often unbelief and idolatry. Read Psalm 106:34-39 (page 463).

What led to Israel's downfall?

What act of disobedience led Israel to adultery?

It's shocking, isn't it? Sadly, if we take a close look at today's culture, our own practices when held up to God's standards are just as shocking. The only difference is that our culture is familiar to us—we're *used* to our culture, so we don't see the activities, philosophies, and practices as idols that conflict with our relationship with God. Nonetheless, they are. And they are just as terrible.

What are some examples of idolatry that you recognize in our culture?

What solutions would you suggest for overcoming those idols in your life?

The Blessings of Knowing God

Read Psalm 16:5 (page 419).

How does David describe the Lord?

In David's mind, focused as it was on God, nothing came close to the inheritance he had in Him. He also described the Lord as *"my cup of blessing."*

What does he mean by that?

Let's look up some of the blessings the Bible tells us are ours through our relationship with God. Record what each passage says are the blessings of being God's children.

2 Peter 1:3-4 (page 938)

James 1:17 (page 930)

Psalm 5:12 (page 416)

Ephesians 1:3 (page 895)

2 Corinthians 1:22 (page 882)

1 John 1:9 (page 941)

Philippians 4:13 (page 901)

1 Peter 1:4-5 (page 934)

In Psalm 16:5, what does David say God does for him?

On more than one occasion David lost things that were precious to him, but still he trusted God, knowing where his true treasure was. A wonderful verse about how God guards us is Philippians 4:7 (page 901).

How is God's peace described?

What parts of us are protected by God's peace?

Think about that for a moment. If our heart and our mind are protected, does anything else matter?

Think of a situation where you or someone you know experienced God's peace at such a level it couldn't be explained.

Another verse along this line is Ephesians 3:17 (page 896). What happens as our roots grow deep into the love of God?

Read Psalm 16:7 (page 419).

The word *bless* is synonymous with praise, and one thing David did well was praise God. Praise is not just something we do orally; we also praise God through our actions. For example, how do the following verses tell us to praise Him?

Matthew 5:16 (page 736)

John 15:8 (page 824)

Romans 15:5-6 (page 868)

It's absolutely true that actions speak louder than words. The main reason the words *Christian* and *hypocrite* have become associated in the world's eyes is because our actions as Christians often don't live up to our words. The best way to bless God, to give Him honor and praise, is to live lives that accurately reflect Jesus.

> *Be careful to live properly*
> *among your unbelieving neighbors.*
> —1 Peter 2:12a (page 935)

And let's not forget the last phrase of Psalm 16:7 (page 419). Since we talked about meditation and memorization in the first chapter, we won't talk more, but just remind yourself of this wonderful fact.

True Security

Psalm 16:8 is one of the most reassuring verses in the Bible. Verse 9 goes along with it, so let's read them together.

Where does David's sense of security come from?

What makes you feel secure?

A sense of security can be elusive, and yet it's one of the basic human cravings. We crave material security, but a "just a little more" mentality keeps it beyond our fingertips. We crave relational security, but tiny questions arise when least expected and torment us with doubt. We crave security in regard to our future, but there are no guarantees to be found in the unknown.

David knew his only true security was found in God. Wealth disappears, people disappoint, and the future dissolves, but God is steady and true—always there, always guarding our heart and our mind.

Insecurity is most likely to flare up when it comes to making decisions that will impact our future. How can we be sure we're making the right decision? David faced this question many times as king, and his decisions were much further reaching than ours. They affected everyone in the kingdom! Here, especially, it is to our advantage to align ourselves with God—utilizing His promise of wisdom. Read James 1:5 (page 930).

What do the following verses have to say in regard to feeling secure as we make decisions?

Psalm 25:4-5 (page 424)

Psalm 27:11 (page 425)

Psalm 73:24 (page 446)

Isaiah 30:21 (pages 539-540)

Proverbs 3:5-6 (page 482)

Any of these verses would be excellent to memorize, but if you want to choose just one, Proverbs 3:5-6 is a wonderful summarization of them all. Write it onto a 3x5 card and keep it handy for easy reference.

A Prophecy of Resurrection

The last part of this psalm switches from a personal prayer to a prophecy about Jesus' resurrection.

Read Psalm 16:8-11 (page 420).

The apostles Peter and Paul both quoted this passage in sermons they preached hundreds of years later in the New Testament.

Read part of Peter's sermon in Jerusalem in Acts 2:25-32 (page 831).

Paul also quotes Psalm 16 in the sermon he gave in the synagogue at Antioch. Read Acts 13:34-37 (page 842).

Jesus died for our sins, but He did not stay dead. What do the following verses say about His resurrection?

Matthew 16:21 (page 747)

Acts 10:39-41 (page 839)

Romans 1:4 (page 857)

Ephesians 1:19-20 (page 895)

The very same power that defied death, God has made available to us today! What do the following verses teach us about the resurrection of those who believe in Christ?

John 6:40 (page 814)

John 11:25 (page 820)

2 Corinthians 4:14 (page 884)

1 Thessalonians 4:16-18 (page 906)

The fact that Jesus died for our sins and was then resurrected—the fact that He lives this very moment in the hearts of believers—is why these final verses of Psalm 16 also apply to us. God will show us the way of life, granting us the joy of His presence and the pleasures of living with Him forever (Psalm 16:11)!

──────── *Personal Reflection and Application* ────────

From this chapter,

I see…

I believe…

I will…

Prayer

Lord, it is so good to be near you! I have made you my shelter, and I will tell everyone about the wonderful things you do. O Lord, you are so good, so ready to forgive, and so full of unfailing love for all who ask for your help (Psalm 73:28, page 446, and Psalm 86:5, page 453).

──────── *Thoughts, Notes, and Prayer Requests* ────────

_____

_____

_____

_____

_____

_____

_____

_____

5

Christ—Our Crucified, Risen Savior
Psalm 22

Our son Tyler was eight years old when he accepted Jesus as his Savior at a church camp meeting. Everyone was very excited and we were all hugging and congratulating him. Afterward, walking back to our cabin, his brother, Landon, who'd made the same decision a year earlier, asked Tyler how he felt now. "I have a stomachache!" Tyler complained.

"Well," Landon explained knowingly, "that's probably because when your sin left your heart it went to your stomach."

His theology was a bit skewed, but he was right on the important part—that Tyler's sin had left his heart. When we accept Jesus as our Savior, our sin, in God's mind, is gone. It's as if it never happened!

Prayer

God, thank you for forgiving my sins and never again remembering them. Thank you for removing them from my life as far as the east is from the west (Hebrews 8:12, page 924, and Psalm 103:12, page 460).

The Non-Abandoning God

The psalm we are focusing on in this chapter is Psalm 22. However, there is another psalm for us to look at first to establish some perspective. Read Psalm 139:1-18 (page 476).

As you read, jot down all the things God knows about you and all the places He follows you.

Quite a list, isn't it? What does this tell you about God's level of interest in you?

Let's look at two more verses along this line. Read Hebrews 13:5-6 (page 928).

In light of what we've just read, is there any place you can go where God won't follow?

Is there any time in your life when God will abandon you?

Now, keeping this incredible knowledge in mind, turn to Psalm 22 (pages 422-423). This is the most noted of the messianic psalms—*messianic* meaning "having to do with the Messiah." If you remember, *Messiah* is one of the titles for Jesus, and it means "the Anointed One" or "the Chosen One." And the word *Christ* is from the Greek word for *Messiah*, so *Christ* and *Messiah* mean the same thing.

More than any other psalm, this one, written at least a thousand years before Jesus was killed, clearly and graphically describes His crucifixion. Crucifixion was a Roman method of capital punishment.

It opens with the most agonizing words imaginable. *"My God, my God, why have you abandoned me?"* These are the very words Jesus cried out after hanging on the cross for several excruciating hours.

The Bible tells us that Jesus was crucified around 9:00 a.m. Three agonizing hours later, darkness covered the land, and it stayed dark for three hours. Imagine what a terrifying, oppressive time that must have been. Evil had run rampant for hours in the city of Jerusalem, and from all appearances it had achieved its despicable goal. Think of how grief-stricken and hopeless and forsaken by God those who loved Jesus must have felt as the untimely darkness descended. Think even of the ones who believed Jesus deserved to die. With the inexplicable darkness covering the city in the middle of the day, how terrified were they as the sickening realization of the truth gnawed at their thoughts?

Think what it must have been like for Jesus. How often had He taught that He is the light (John 8:12, page 817), but now, in the worst moment of His earthly life, there was utter blackness. Oh, how unbearable the weight of our sin must have seemed as He bore it alone. No wonder He made that terrible cry to His Father.

Have you ever had a time when you truly felt abandoned by God? Please explain.

It's a feeling most everyone has at some point in their life, and David describes that feeling in Psalm 22:2 (page 422).

Can you relate? What is a circumstance you have long cried out to God about—with no relief?

The next section is key to everything! Read Psalm 22:3-5. What did David proclaim in verse 3?

holy one

Yes! He acknowledged God's holiness! He fortified himself by recalling God's unwavering faithfulness in the past! In other words, he changed his thought pattern. Instead of focusing on what he felt was God's abandonment, he contemplated God's holiness and past faithfulness.

How would making this attitude change make a difference in regard to present circumstances in your life?

Even knowing God will never abandon us, there are times when the road we have to walk feels very dark and lonely. That's why we need to memorize verses like the ones we read at the beginning of the chapter, so we can pull them out of our minds and draw comfort from them when our circumstances seem unbearable. Because the truth is this—if you belong to God, He will never abandon you!

Remarkable Prophecies

The following chart lists the prophecies given in Psalm 22 about Jesus' death and the fulfillment of each prophecy in the New Testament. Read the scriptures listed in the two outside columns and note the prophecy that was fulfilled in the center column. The first one we have already looked at.

Prophecies Concerning Christ

Prophecy Verses	Prophecy and Fulfillment	Fulfillment Verses
Psalm 22:1	*Why did you desert me*	Mark 15:34 (page 777)
Psalm 22:6-8	*why doesn't he is the son of God*	Matthew 27:41-43 (pages 759-760)
Psalm 22:12-13		Matthew 27:39-40 (page 759)
Psalm 22:15		John 19:28 (page 827)
Psalm 22:16		John 19:37 and John 20:25,27 (page 828)
Psalm 22:17		Matthew 27:36 (page 759)
Psalm 22:18		John 19:23-24 (page 827)

Perhaps one of the most miraculous prophecies about Jesus' death is found in Psalm 34:20 (page 428), which says no bone will be broken in His body. Read the fulfillment in John 19:31-33 (page 827).

Add to that the fact that the spikes used to nail Him to the cross missed all 27 bones that make up the hand and wrist!

Psalm 22:14-18 describes in detail the physical toll the crucifixion took on Jesus' body.

Focusing on God

In verses 19-23 we see a repeat of what occurred in verses 1-5. Read verses 19-21. What is David asking for?

Now read verses 24-25. What does he immediately switch to?

Yes! Once again, he chooses to fix his focus on God and praise Him for all He has done.

Read Psalm 22:27-31.

Who will acknowledge the Lord and return to Him?

What do you feel is most important about this section?

According to this passage, is there anyone who will not eventually acknowledge Jesus as God?

This is reiterated in the New Testament in Romans 14:11 (page 867). How does this verse compare to the end of Psalm 22?

Psalm 22, more than any other, is the psalm of the cross. It shows, with great sweeping emotion, what happened at the cross and what was accomplished there. Read the first and last verse again.

What a sacred contrast these two verses portray—from the worst possible agony that had all the appearances of defeat to the ongoing victorious outcome. God cannot and will not be defeated. Align yourself fully with Him.

─────────── *Personal Reflection and Application* ───────────

From this chapter,

I see…

I believe…

I will…

───────────── ✑ ─────────────

Prayer

Lord, thank you that I belong to you and have become a new person. My old life is gone; a new life has begun! You have saved me and called me to live a holy life. You did this not because I deserved it, but because that was your plan from before the beginning of time—to show me your grace through Christ Jesus (2 Corinthians 5:17, page 884, and 2 Timothy 1:9, page 914).

─────────── *Thoughts, Notes, and Prayer Requests* ───────────

_____

_____

_____

_____

_____

_____

Christ—Our Shepherd and Gracious Host

Psalm 23

P salm 23 is the best-known of all the psalms in the Bible. Only six verses long, its quiet, simple message has comforted and strengthened countless people in countless situations.

In the book *Let's Roll*, Lisa Beamer recounts the numbing horror of the days following the terrorist attack on September 11, 2001. Her husband, Todd, was on United Flight 93, which crashed into a Pennsylvania field after the passengers rushed the cockpit and thwarted the plans of the terrorists who had hijacked the plane.

Several days after the tragedy, Lisa learned that Todd had made a phone call to a GTE Airfone supervisor before the plane crashed. When she met the woman over the phone, it was like a "phone call from Heaven," because the supervisor told her everything her husband had said in his final moments of life. She told Lisa that just before the passengers rushed the cockpit, Todd asked her to pray the Lord's Prayer with him. When they finished, Todd recited the Twenty-Third Psalm. The supervisor told Lisa there was a sigh in his voice as he completed the psalm, and then he took a deep breath and uttered the words no one will ever forget: "Are you ready? Okay, let's roll!"

Todd Beamer's final words are proof of God's power working through the words of the Twenty-Third Psalm, not only to comfort but to also infuse us with otherwise inexplicable strength and courage.*

∞

Prayer

Lord, I see how much you love me, for you call me your child, and that is what I am! I will be strong and courageous! I will not be afraid and will not panic. For you, my God will personally go ahead of me. You will neither fail me nor abandon me (1 John 3:1a, page 942, and Deuteronomy 31:6, page 163).

God Meets All of Our Needs

All of God's Word has the power to bring immense comfort, but Psalm 23 heads the list of comforting passages.

It draws a beautiful analogy between a shepherd and his sheep and Jesus and His followers. Interestingly, it does not include a single plea, request, or even praise. It is simply a description of what life is like when we follow Jesus. The most notable aspect of this psalm is that every single verse tells us at least one thing God does for us, and most verses tell us more than one thing. Read Psalm 23 (page 423) and make note of what each verse says God does.

1.

2.

---

* Lisa Beamer, *Let's Roll!* (Wheaton, IL: Tyndale House Publishers, Inc., 2002), pp. 211-214.

3.

4.

5.

6.

When you look back over your list, is there any need you have that is not addressed in this psalm? As our shepherd, Jesus is not only aware of our needs, but He makes sure they're provided—even without our asking.

Look at the first verse again. Did you notice that *Lord* is in all caps? If you remember, that is the translation of *Yahweh*, God's personal name, which means self-existent and everlasting. This name always refers to God's absolute faithfulness to His people. However, the full Hebrew form in this psalm is Yahweh-Rohi, which means "the Lord my Shepherd." David describes Jesus as his shepherd right at the beginning. What does the last phrase of verse 1 say?

"All that I need!" If only we could fully grasp the truth of that phrase. In Jesus, we have all we will ever need. He is our *Yahweh-Rohi*—our All-sufficient One, our Shepherd. Is there a need in your life that you feel is not being met? Offer it up to the Lord in prayer. Ask Him to show you this need from *His* perspective.

Open up your hands and tell God you trust Him with this area of your life. Tell Him that you're choosing to trust His timing and His provision. Thank Him for where you are right now in regard to this need and what you're learning through it.

The Heart of the Shepherd

David isn't the only psalm writer who referred to Jesus as our Shepherd. How does Jesus act like a shepherd in each of these passages?

Psalm 78:52 (page 449)

Psalm 79:13 (page 450)

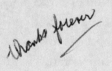

What makes Psalm 23 with its analogy of a shepherd and his sheep so meaningful is the fact that David was an expert when it came to sheep. He was an expert on shepherding. He had the heart and mind of a shepherd. He knew exactly how a shepherd felt about his flock. He also was intimately acquainted with the ways of sheep—he knew their strengths and weaknesses. He knew what caused them to thrive and what caused them to fail. This is not some random analogy David grabbed out of thin air; it is an analogy he was born into, one that he lived!

Even though this psalm applies to everyone, it is actually a very personal psalm David wrote, using only personal pronouns. What was it that he knew about sheep that made him compare himself to one? Other experts on sheep tell us that

- sheep are the most helpless of all animals

- sheep have no sense of direction—they cannot find their way home

- sheep are defenseless, with no claws or teeth, no natural camouflage, and an inability to run very fast

- sheep are helpless when injured—most animals lick their wounds, but a sheep relies on its shepherd for care

These attributes of sheep (being almost totally helpless) explain why David chose them for an analogy of his relationship with God. It shows how fully and completely he had come to trust in the Lord. He had come to recognize God as *Yahweh-Rohi*—his all-sufficient God and Shepherd.

It is important to put David's dependence on God in perspective. He was not in any way a weak, timid man. Dependence was not a natural characteristic of his. In reality, he was fearless. Read 1 Samuel 17:34-40 (page 224).

Lions and bears with only a club? Does that sound like a helpless person who's unable to defend himself? This passage of Scripture is from when David was insisting that King Saul let him face the giant Goliath, who had all the other soldiers in terror. David went out to face Goliath with only a shepherd's staff, bag of five stones, and a slingshot. What David learned as a shepherd and later, as king, was the faithfulness of God. David's faith was strengthened.

There is one other interesting piece of information about sheep. They are unable to clean themselves as other animals can. A sheep remains dirty until the shepherd cleans it. In this way too, David drew a perfect analogy, knowing that only God could clean up his heart. Read Psalm 51:10-12 (page 436).

David wrote this prayer of wholehearted repentance after his immoral affair with Bathsheba and the murder of her husband.

What did he ask God to do in the very last phrase?

As passionate as David was about his relationship with God, he still made extremely poor choices sometimes. In fact, he went down in history for a couple of his more notable sins. But he acknowledged his sin to God and did what was necessary to get his life back on the right path. He recognized his weak areas and asked God to change his heart and make him willing to follow God's path.

What are the weak areas in your life? In what situations are you most likely to make the wrong choices?

Ask God to make you willing to turn away from this part of your life. Tell Him that you want to follow His path instead of your own.

Trusting God to Lead Us

Sheep also have some good traits, and here David's analogy fits his relationship with God as well. For example:

- Sheep do not have to be marked or branded. If several flocks of sheep are mingled together, each flock will follow their own shepherd when he calls them to leave.

- Sheep instinctively trust the shepherd to provide for them.

What are some ways we can become more natural at trusting God to provide for us?

One of the best ways for our trust to become more instinctual is through Scripture meditation and memorization. The more familiar we become with God, the more natural our trust will become. The Bible is full of His promises to guide us. Look up the following verses and note what they say.

Psalm 32:8 (page 427)

Which pathway does God say He will guide us on?

Think about this. The Bible tells us that God knows everything—including what is going to happen tomorrow and ten years from tomorrow. We don't know what is going to happen beyond this precise second. So who is in the best position to know which path we should take? What do the following verses say?

Psalm 48:14 (page 435)

Proverbs 3:5 (page 482)

Isaiah 58:11 (page 563)

John 16:12-15 (pages 824-825)

Galatians 5:16-18 (page 893)

How is the Holy Spirit's guidance in the New Testament related to God's guidance mentioned in the Old Testament?

Describe a time you had a very clear sense of being led by God.

David had learned to trust God's guidance.

What was the result of God's guiding David along right paths, according to Psalm 23:2-3 (page 423)?

Experience has taught us, though, that not every place God leads us is peaceful. In verse 4, David acknowledges that God sometimes leads him through the darkest valley. What was David's response when He did that?

These aren't just words he's writing to make a good poem. These are words he has lived. Read 1 Samuel 30:3-6 (page 233).

There is something heart-wrenching about the image of warriors weeping inconsolably. David wept with his men too because his family was among those captured. But he also carried the crushing burden of blame for this terrible tragedy—so much so that his men wanted him dead.

But what does the end of verse 6 say David did?

How do you think he did this?

Comfort from the Shepherd

Moving back to Psalm 23, did you notice the subtle change in verse 4 that continued for the rest of the psalm? In verses 1 through 3, David spoke of God in the third person. He switched from speaking about God to speaking directly to God when he started to talk about going through difficult seasons of life. Why do you think David did this?

Comfort is a universal human need, and much of the Bible is given to comforting and encouraging believers. The rod and staff that David refers to is a picturesque description of comfort. A shepherd used his rod to number the sheep as they came in or went out of the sheepfold. He noticed each sheep and called them by name as they passed under his rod—just as Jesus notices each of us and calls us by name as He takes care of our needs. The crook at the end of the shepherd's staff was used to rescue a sheep in danger or to help it over a brook or difficult spot. The staff was also used to strike predators and keep them away from the sheep. In every way, David's analogy of Jesus as a shepherd and us as sheep is perfect. With it he paints a beautiful picture of the relationship between Jesus and His followers.

Why do you think God doesn't prevent the difficult and tragic circumstances that come into our life?

Jesus said, *"I have told you all this so that you may have peace in me. Here on earth you will have many trials and sorrows. But take heart, because I have overcome the world"* (John 16:33, page 825).

God doesn't interfere with our free will; and many of the difficult and tragic circumstances we experience are the result of someone's misuse of their free will, such as rape, abuse, or drunk driving. Some circumstances are simply the result of life on a sin-afflicted earth—such as natural disasters or disease.

But the tremendous advantage of a personal relationship with Jesus when such things occur is that we do not endure them alone. God gives us supernatural comfort and peace. He brings His power to bear in our lives and keeps His promise to work through the tragedy to make us a stronger, better person. Only He has the power to accomplish something good from a tragedy or terrible injustice. Read the following verses and note what they say:

Genesis 50:20 (page 43)

Romans 8:28-29 (page 863)

Read the following verses. What are some things that can result from difficult circumstances?

Romans 5:3-4 (page 860)

Philippians 1:12-14 (page 899)

Psalm 50:15 (page 436)

Whether or not we ultimately benefit from difficult circumstances is up to us, based on how we choose to respond. Even in this, God does not force us. We choose whether we will become hardened and bitter or soft and yielding in His hands. While He does not force us, He will help us. When bitterness or anger overpowers us and chokes the life out of us, if we ask, He will help us break it down into manageable portions that we can deal with—and eventually dispose of it altogether. God wants us to experience abundant life, and if we stay focused on Him, He will make it possible—regardless of circumstances. That's the advantage of a relationship with Him.

God—Our Loving, Loyal Host

In Psalm 23:5 David makes an interesting change in analogies—as poets sometimes do. He changes from a shepherd and his sheep to a host and his guest. Read verse 5.

Did you notice the rather unusual location where the feast takes place? How would you explain the reasons behind God preparing a feast for David in front of his enemies?

Here again, David's analogy, even though it has changed, makes the same point. In the loving care of Jesus we are safe—in fact we can even throw a party! Surrounded by enemies (difficult circumstances) our cup (life) can still overflow with blessings. Only a relationship with God can make that sense of security a reality!

I love the wording in the final verse of Psalm 23. What does it say about God's goodness and unfailing love?

Oh! Isn't that incredible and wonderful? His love *pursues* us! How would you define the word *pursue*?

If you check it out in a thesaurus you will find words with a similar meaning, such as *chase, track, shadow, follow*—even *hound*! God's love will *hound* us all the days of our lives. We cannot escape His goodness or His love. How does that truth impact your life?

You can see now why Psalm 23 is such a loved psalm. David's analogy of a shepherd and his sheep is a beautiful portrayal of our relationship with Jesus. But are you ready for the most exciting part of this analogy? More than a thousand years later, when Jesus walked on this earth, He chose this very same analogy to describe His love and care for us. Read John 10:1-15 (page 819).

To know more about accepting the wonderful life God is offering you, see "Know God" on pages 177-179.

Do you see how loved you are by God? What did Jesus say His purpose was in verse 10?

The question you have to ask yourself then is, will you accept the rich and satisfying life Jesus is offering you?

———— *Personal Reflection and Application* ————

From this chapter,

I see…

I believe…

I will…

Prayer

God, you have said that if I confess with my mouth that Jesus is Lord and believe in my heart that God raised Him from the dead, I will be saved. Right now, in spite of questions, I choose to believe in my heart that I have been made right with God, and I am confessing with my mouth that I have been saved (Romans 10:9-10, page 864).

Thoughts, Notes, and Prayer Requests

_____

_____

_____

_____

_____

_____

_____

_____

_____

_____

_____

_____

_____

_____

_____

_____

_____

_____

_____

_____

_____

_____

_____

_____

_____

7

A Christlike Attitude
Psalm 40

Y ou have to be patient!" If my mother said that to me once, she said it a hundred times—and I didn't like it any more the hundredth time than I did the first. Jobs that require patience have always presented an extra challenge to me. Take, for instance, laying tile.

One day I decided to tackle this job on the walls and floor of our bathroom. I knew nothing about laying tile, but I had a wonderfully patient friend who was willing to teach me. Ed was an exceedingly careful man who left nothing to chance. Patience *defined* him. He instructed me in everything he thought I could ever possibly need to know about tiling—the key instruction being "You can't rush a tile job."

However, we had company coming in a few days, and I wanted the tile job finished before their arrival. Instead of moving slowly as Ed had recommended, I laid the tile straight up the wall, row upon heavy row, as fast as I could. Even working as fast as I was, it seemed slow. About midnight, I went to bed exhausted, with only half the job done.

About 3:00 a.m. I woke up from a terrible dream in which all my hastily laid tile had slid off the wall. I flew into the bathroom and discovered that my tile, although it hadn't slid completely off the wall, had buckled on itself. It all had to be removed. I tucked my night-gown around my legs and went to work scraping off all the mud and *patiently* reapplying tiles as Ed had taught me.

I learned two things from that awful chapter:

1. It pays to do things right the first time.

2. God is merciful. If He hadn't caused me to wake up at 3:00 a.m., the tile mud would have been much more set by morning. It would have been very difficult and costly to remove them and begin all over again.

Developing a Christlike attitude (which involves patience) saves us so much heartache in the long run. It *does* pay to do things right the first time, and developing the attitude of Christ is the right thing to do.

❦

Prayer

God, I know that I never have to be afraid because you are with me. I never have to be discouraged, because you are my God. You have promised to strengthen, help, and hold me up with your victorious right hand. Thank you that your power will produce the endurance and patience that I need, and I will be filled with joy (Isaiah 41:10, page 548, and Colossians 1:11, page 902).

Waiting for God's Help

Psalm 40 (pages 431-432) is a psalm of praise to God. David wrote it about his own experiences, but it has a powerful spiritual applica-tion for us, as well. Let's start by reading the first three verses.

What six things did David say happened when he waited patiently for the Lord to help him?

1. Set me on a rock

2. a song

3. delivered me from the pit

4. patients

5. he heard my cry

6.

Wow! It's enough to make you want to work on developing patience, isn't it? In what areas do you struggle with having patience?

The Bible has a lot to say about prayerfully waiting for the Lord's help. Read the following verses and note what comes from waiting patiently.

Psalm 62:5 (page 440)

hope & rest

Psalm 62:1-2 (page 440)

strength

Psalm 59:9 (page 439)

Isaiah 40:31 (page 548)

Romans 8:23-25 (page 862)

Romans 15:4-5 (page 868)

Victory, rescue, renewed strength! Wonderful benefits come from waiting on God. When we remember that He sees all of time—past, present, and future—then it becomes logical to wait for His timing. His knowledge of the future gives Him a perspective we can never have.

Psalm 40:2 says that God lifted David out of his pit of despair and set his feet on solid ground. Not only that, but God steadied him as he walked.

God is our solid ground, our rock and foundation. When we trust in Him, He raises us up from the pit of sin and sets us on His foundation, which can never be shaken. Several times throughout the Bible, He is referred to as a rock or foundation to His people. Read the following verses and note what they say:

Deuteronomy 32:3-4 (page 164)   *Rock & song*

Psalm 27:5 (page 425)

Rock

Luke 6:46-49 (page 787)

Rock

Sometimes life can feel like quicksand, can't it? We don't know what tomorrow holds, or even the next minute. Our only security is in God. If our foundation is in Him, it doesn't matter what tomorrow holds because He has promised to be there with us.

An Attitude of Praise

Psalm 40:3 talks about the new song God gives us to sing—a song of praise. My son and daughter-in-law, instead of praying at mealtime, each say two things they are thankful for and then they complete the following sentence: "My life is filled with good things because ___*Jesus*___." It's their way of singing a song of praise. Just for fun, write your own song of praise using their pattern.

An attitude of praise and thanksgiving is vital to our well-being! It transforms our attitude as it switches our focus from our circumstance to God. God longs to hear us praise Him. Even more importantly, He *deserves* to hear us praise Him. Read the following Bible verses that praise God:

Psalm 33:4-5 (page 427) *Love*
Psalm 96:2 (page 457)
Psalm 98:1 (page 458) *with victory*

The Bible is *full* of praise to God. This is just a minute sample. Imagine memorizing one of those praises and repeating it to God throughout the day. For example, what if you went through the day reminding yourself of the first two verses we just read—that you can trust everything God does because His unfailing love fills the earth? How differently do you think you would process the events of your day if they were filtered through that perspective of praise?

Shall we experiment? Choose one of the above verses—or one of your own choosing, as long as it's a praise—and repeat it to yourself this week every single time something happens that brings a negative response in you. If someone tailgates you on the way home, replace your irritated thought with the verse of your choice. If your manager is bossy or your neighbor is rude, remind yourself of your verse before you respond. Notice how this changes you, and perhaps your attitude toward that person.

Can you remember a time when you prayed and waited for the Lord's help? What did you learn about God during that waiting period?

Transformation and Trust

Look back at the latter part of Psalm 40:3. What will be the result when people see what God has done for you?

When Jesus transforms a life, there is a noticeable change. You think and behave differently. It is amazing to see someone whose response to life circumstances goes against normal human nature. Someone whose life has been transformed can be a powerful pointer to God for other people.

Take some time to examine your life and determine whether there are any areas in which you have hindered God from working.

In what way are you most likely *not* painting a picture of transformation?

Ask God right now to help you with this area of your life. Remember, David asked God to make him want to live the right way. Read Psalm 40:4.

This verse talks about the joys we have when we trust in the Lord instead of idols. In David's culture, people worshipped countless idols, trusting in their power to give them a good life. These idols were often nothing more than metal, wood, stone, or clay objects, but people nonetheless "trusted" in them. It seems silly to think about, viewed from today's culture, but the fact is that our culture has its own idols. What would you say some modern-day idols are?

We trust money to give us security. We trust fitness and beauty to give us self-confidence. We trust entertainment to free us from worries. We trust self-development to give us wisdom. When you think about it, we're no different from the people in David's day, are we? None of these things will give us joy. They may provide a welcome distraction or happiness for a limited time, but ultimately they will lead to gnawing emptiness. Trusting in God is the only pathway to the joy people are so desperately seeking through the idols of today's culture.

A New Song of Praise

We can use Psalm 40:5 as another template for writing a "new song" of praise. It is a little more detailed than the one we wrote earlier, but let's try our hand at it. There are four sentences in this verse so let's take them one at a time and see where we end up.

"O LORD, my God, you have performed many wonders for us."

List five wonders God has performed. (In case you need an example of a wonder, think of how the sun rises every single morning.)

1.

2.

3.

4.

5.

end

"Your plans for us are too numerous to list."

List three of God's plans you have personally seen come to fruition.

1. family

2. health   Christian life

3. Chad family

"You have no equal."

List four of the biggest false religions/gods you can think of that are *nothing* compared to God.

1. idols

2.

3.

4.

*"If I tried to recite all your wonderful deeds, I would never come to the
end of them."*

List five wonderful deeds God has done for you personally.

1. *Savior*

2. *U.S.A.*

3. *Christian Parents*

4.

5.

There! You've just written another praise song. Every week or so, try
writing a new praise psalm, using a variety of this pattern—or develop
your own pattern. God loves to hear your praise!

Taking Joy in Doing His Will

Psalm 40:6-8 shows how fully David had come to understand
what God desires of us. Read these verses and jot down a thought
or question that comes to mind.

During Old Testament times, people who came to God brought a sacrifice. The sacrifice was a symbol representing an innocent substitute dying in the place of one who sinned. Sin's penalty was death. Those who brought the sacrificial animal confessed their sins, and the animal was killed, giving its life in place of the sinner.

Sacrifices of the Old Testament were to illustrate the fact that God would provide an innocent substitute, who would die in our place and thus pay the penalty for our sin. That was Jesus' purpose in coming to earth. He, who was God in the flesh, was our perfect sacrifice. He put an end to any need for more sacrifices. He has taken away sin once for all, rather than temporarily covering it as the Old Testament sacrifices did. Read Hebrews 10:1-18 (pages 925-926).

What is the first thing David says in Psalm 40:6?

If sacrifices were the way to show repentance in the Old Testament, why do you think David said God took no delight in them?

This is what David had come to understand from his close walk with God. True repentance means you have changed. *Your behavior changes.* People who kept doing the same thing over and over, making the same wrong choices and then bringing a sacrifice so they could start out with a clean slate before God were not truly repentant. God knew it. He took no pleasure in those sacrifices because they were meaningless.

We don't offer sacrifices today but the same truth applies. True repentance means we have changed. If we keep doing the same thing over and over again and keep asking God's forgiveness, we may be fooling ourselves, but we surely are not fooling God. God sees our heart and He recognizes when we want to do His will. Verse 8 shows David's fully repentant spirit when he says *"I take joy in doing your will."* David offers God the sacrifice of obedience to His will.

David had discovered the pure joy of exchanging his desires for God's desires. It's what Jesus is talking about in John 14:15 (page 823) and John 15:14 (page 824).

What does He say? *holy spirit - Obey*

There is no better, more satisfying way to live than by following God's plan for living. Absolutely none! Let's take a moment and ask God to make Psalm 40:8 as true in our lives as it was in David's.

How Wonderful God Is!

Read Psalm 40:9-10.

What are the five characteristics of the Lord that David tells everyone about?

1. *tell everyone*

2. *he didn't hide it*

3. *righteousness*

4.

5.

It sounds like David couldn't keep from telling people about God, doesn't it? I confess, I don't find it quite so easy. How about you? What is your biggest obstacle in talking to people about Jesus?

Write down the name of one person you'd like to talk to about Jesus.

Every day this week, pray for that person. Pray for their needs, pray for their protection, pray for everything you know is important to them. And every day ask God to make their heart open to Him; ask Him to give you an opportunity to talk to them. Perhaps there will be some exciting stories to share.

Read Psalm 40:11 (page 432).

What does this verse say about God's mercy, love, and faithfulness?

don't hold back your love & tenderness protect safe

What response does God's loving mercy inspire in your heart?

secure

Read Psalm 40:12-17.

Developing Patience

Verses 11-13 are quite interesting, and they show just how much we have in common with David, even separated as we are by centuries and cultures. In verse 5, David's blessings were more than he could count. Now his troubles are more than he can count. Isn't that the story of our life sometimes? And as with David, some of our troubles are due to circumstances beyond our control and some are due to our own foolish sins. But oh, how wonderful to know that God's mercy is far greater than our sins!

What is the very last line of Psalm 40:17?

Do you remember what the very first line of this psalm is?

Don't you love it? More importantly, *don't you relate?* From *"I wait patiently,"* to *"do not delay."* Hmm. Do you think the change could have something to do with attitude? In the beginning, David is filled with patience as he reflects on all the Lord has done for him. In the end, he leans toward impatience as he reflects on all his troubles. What do you think—is there a correlation?

yes

How have you seen this play out in your life?

patience

Galatians 5:22-23 (page 893) tell us that the Holy Spirit produces patience in us.

This chapter has given us lots to think about as we consider how we can develop an attitude more like Christ's. Don't forget the two challenges for the week! Do you remember what they are?

1.

2.

──────── *Personal Reflection and Application* ────────

From this chapter,

I see...

I believe...

I will...

❦

Prayer

God, thank you for your glory and excellence that have given me great and precious promises. These are the promises that enable me to share in your divine nature and escape the world's corruption caused by human desires (2 Peter 1:4, page 938).

Thoughts, Notes, and Prayer Requests

8

Christ—The King of Love and Beauty
Psalm 45

Before we begin, how did meditating on a verse of praise affect your attitude since you studied the previous chapter?

And did you have an opportunity to talk to the person you've been praying for?

It's very exciting to put God's Word into practice in our lives, isn't it? He's always eager to help us when we step out in ways that will affect our lives for the better and, at the same time, influence others by the difference they see in us.

Prayer

Lord, I look forward to when we will be caught up in the clouds to meet you in the air so we can be with you forever. I anticipate the prize that awaits me—the crown of righteousness that you, the righteous Judge, are going to give me on the day of your return. And it's not just a prize for me but for everyone who is eagerly looking forward to your appearing (1 Thessalonians 4:17b, page 906, and 2 Timothy 4:8, pages 915-916).

The Royal Wedding

Many people love a wedding, and the psalm we're looking at now describes a beautiful one—but it has not yet taken place. We've already looked at some of the psalms containing prophecies about Jesus that were fulfilled during His life on earth. There are also some psalms containing prophecies about Jesus that haven't been fulfilled yet. Psalm 45 is one of those psalms. Because so many prophecies have already been precisely fulfilled, we can be confident in God, who does not lie, to bring to pass everything He has promised.

Some people believe Psalm 45 was originally the marriage hymn of a Jewish king who was married to a foreign princess. However, there's never been an earthly king who lives up to the description given in this lovely psalm. Early Christian writers and Jewish interpreters agree that this is a messianic psalm referring to when Jesus will return to earth in the future.

It is divided into the following sections:

- Verse 1 is the dedication of the song

- Verses 2-3 describe the bridegroom king

- Verses 4-5 describe the result of his warfare

- Verses 6-9 describe the kingdom

- Verses 10-12 give the bride some advice

- Verses 13-15 describe the entrance of the bride

- Verses 16-17 express the expectation of the marriage

To begin, let's read through all of Psalm 45 (pages 433-434).

Goodness! Did you notice how enthusiastic the author of this psalm is as he describes the bridegroom? He's as enthusiastic as a bride who's anticipating her bridegroom!

As you noticed, verse 1 is simply a preface, stating the author's intent. Verses 2-7 are a description of both the king's physical traits and his character traits.

List the character traits this passage describes:

respental of him

Now list the traits you found that clearly refer to Christ:

fairest
mighty one
your throne
lasts forever

In the Old Testament, the relationship between God and Israel is represented as a marriage. For example, read the following verses:

Isaiah 54:5 (page 560)
Jeremiah 31:32 (page 599)   *being a husband*

In the New Testament, the symbolism is transferred to Christ and His church—*church* referring to Christ's followers. This metaphor appears frequently in the writings of the apostle Paul and in Revelation. John the Baptist also referred to Christ as the Bridegroom. Read John 3:27-30 (page 811).

Even Jesus spoke of Himself as the Groom. One example is Luke 5:33-35 (page 785).

In each case, the bride is referring to the church. Some examples of this are found in the following verses:

Revelation 19:7-9 (page 960)   *bride*
Revelation 22:17 (page 962)   *water of life*
2 Corinthians 11:2 (page 887)

The Conquering King

Psalm 45:4 is a very exciting verse. Remember, this psalm is a prophecy about Jesus that has not yet been fulfilled. What does it say He is riding out to?

Sometimes it's easy to think that our circumstances, both personally and in regard to the condition of the world, are hopeless. Evil is rampant. Morality has been shrugged off. Christianity is mocked. But ultimately, Christ will be the victor. And those who align themselves with Him will experience that victory. How does knowing this impact your attitude when you see evil conquering good in our culture?

Thinking of this in terms of your personal circumstances, where do you feel like you are most hopeless?

Read Romans 8:31-34 (page 863).

Contemplate what you just read. Do you grasp the meaning of the phrase, *"If God is for us, who can ever be against us?"* How do you apply this to your everyday life?

What does verse 32 say?

Rest in the assurance that when you face personal battles the Almighty God, Creator of the Universe, is not only with you—He is for you!

Before we move on, let's look at one more incredible passage of Scripture that fully shows the advantage of being on God's side. The prophet Elisha had angered a king. One morning Elisha and his servant woke up to find themselves in a hopeless situation. Read 2 Kings 6:14-17 (page 287).

Elisha and his servant were surrounded. That was the inescapable fact.

But what did Elisha tell his servant to do in verse 16?

don't be afraid

This is *always* the case. Regardless of how big your problem is, God is bigger! No matter how many problems surround you, He is greater. Why don't we stop for a minute right now and thank Him for this wonderful truth!

The Coming Reign of Christ

Now back to Psalm 45, what is Jesus fighting for according to verses 4-7?

How does your life defend truth, humility, and justice as mentioned in verse 4?

Read John 14:6 (page 823). What is the only way to reach God?

This is where people go terribly wrong. They buy into the philosophy that there are many ways to God. That is a devastating lie with horrifying consequences. There is only one way to Him.

Psalm 45:3-5 symbolizes the victorious second coming of Jesus—the King of Glory as described in Revelation 19:11-16 (page 960).

Psalm 45:6-7 describes what the reign of Christ will be like. This passage is also quoted in Hebrews 1:8-9 (page 920), showing that this psalm is referring to Jesus.

How long does it say Jesus will reign?

How does it describe His reign?

It sounds like something to look forward to, doesn't it? No more corruption, just God's merciful justice. And over all of it is poured joy!

God has promised joy to His believers. Read the following verses and note what they say regarding joy:

Psalm 16:11 (page 420)

Psalm 30:11 (page 426)

John 15:10-11 (page 824)

Romans 14:16-17 (page 867)

When we walk with God, we can experience joy even in difficult circumstances, but when Christ returns, our joy will be without limit and without end.

Leaving the Past Behind

So far, we've only read about the bridegroom. Now let's see what it says about the bride. Read Psalm 45:9-15 (page 434).

Once again, the psalmist is filled with enthusiasm as he describes her. You can tell He enjoys writing about this wedding!

In verse 10, what is the bride told to do?

dont worry about your parents

Why do you think she is given this advice?

forget the past

Again, this is symbolic of what we are to do when we come to Christ—forget our past! It no longer has control over us. Our past no longer defines us. Read 2 Corinthians 5:17 (page 884).

When we begin a relationship with Christ, our past is wiped away in His eyes. He sees none of our failures, none of our sins—nothing but a brand-new person. Read Hebrews 8:12 (page 924).

But if you remember, verse 10 in Psalm 45 wasn't talking about God forgetting our past—it's talking about *us* forgetting our past. There is nothing to be gained from looking backward. In fact, there is much to be lost. If we keep ourselves buried in regret, shame, bitterness, or any other emotion stirred up by our past, we cannot move forward. We cannot become the new person described in Hebrews. If God is willing to forget our past, shouldn't we do the same?

What part of your past are you unable to let go of?

Pretend you are holding it in your hands. Hold it up and show it to God. Tell Him how it makes you feel and why you can't move past it.

Now, open up your hands and let go of it. See it dropping to the floor and rolling far away from you—so far it leaves your range of vision. Thank God for removing the power it's held over you. Thank Him for replacing it with *His* power, which will enable you to move forward in victory. If you like, record your thoughts below.

The advice given to the bride in Psalm 45:10-11 is reiterated throughout the New Testament. Read the following examples:

Colossians 3:1-2 (page 903) *minds focused on her*
Titus 2:11-12 (page 917) *revealed to all mankind*
Romans 12:2 (page 866) *do not do as the World*
1 John 2:15-17 (page 942)
→ *Conform to God*

What do you feel is most important from these passages?

forget the past.

If you put Christ's teaching into practice, what difference do you think it will make in the quality of your life?

Think of this. If you want a successful marriage, will you hang on to your old girlfriends or boyfriends? Of course not—and if you try to, things get complicated and ugly very fast. Some people, when they commit themselves to Christ, still try to hang on to old habits and seek the same pleasures. They try to maintain their old life while living their new life. It's exactly like trying to maintain a relationship with someone you dated while building a new relationship with your spouse. It simply doesn't work. It has to be all or nothing.

The beauty of living our lives fully by Jesus' standards is that the short-term pleasure that comes from living by our own standards is replaced by unshakable joy and incomparable satisfaction. Jesus' love for us is all-consuming, and He richly rewards our commitment to Him. Note down what some of His rewards are in the following verses:

Matthew 7:21 (page 738)

What the father Wants

James 1:25 (page 930)

Keep attending

John 14:23 (page 823)

love you
will Obey me

God rewards our faithfulness to Him in countless ways. He surrounds us with His love, protection, peace, wisdom—everything we need. And one day, Jesus is going to return and the blessings we experience now will be nothing compared to the blessings we will experience when we're face to face with Him as His beloved bride for all eternity!

Joining the Celebration

You can be sure you are part of Christ's bride. The Bible tells us in Romans 3:23 (page 859) and Romans 6:23 (page 861) that we are all sinners and the consequence of our sin is death—forever separated from God. But when Christ came to earth as a man, His purpose was to pay the price for our sins, to die in our place. Jesus' death and resurrection three days later, made it possible for us to have a relationship with God. Read John 1:12-13 (page 809).

Our belief in God's Son, Jesus, means God sees us as His children and that we will have eternal life with Him. If you would like to become a child of God right now, it is simple. Just tell Jesus your thoughts. If you like, you can use the following prayer as a guideline:

> *Jesus, I do believe you are the Son of God and that you died on the cross to pay the penalty for my sin. Please forgive my sin, and make me a part of the family of God. Come into my life and take control of it. Thank you for your gift of eternal life and for your Holy Spirit, who has come to live in me. I ask this in your name. Amen.*

If you just prayed this prayer, you are now part of God's family. You will find over time God will become more and more important to you.

Don't keep your decision a secret! Share the good news with someone, so they can celebrate with you.

Isn't it fun when a wedding invitation arrives in your mail? Sometimes the invitation gives hints about the wedding—what the colors will be, whether it will be casual or formal. It's always pleasant to look forward to being part of the celebration. God mailed everyone a wedding invitation when He sent His Son, Jesus, to die for our sins. He wants us to be looking forward in anticipation to the Bridegroom's arrival, ready to be part of the greatest celebration ever held.

—————— *Personal Reflection and Application* ——————

From this chapter,

I see…

I believe…

I will…

Prayer

Lord, I am looking forward with great anticipation to when you, yourself will come down from heaven with a commanding shout…and together with all other Christians, I will be caught up in the clouds to meet you in the air. Then we will be with you forever (1 Thessalonians 4:16-17, page 906).

Thoughts, Notes, and Prayer Requests

9

Christ—The Faithful God
Psalm 89

One of my dear friends remembers exactly where she was when the United States was attacked on September 11, 2001. As the mother of a baby boy and a five-year-old little girl, she, like all of us, knew our world would never be the same. And while this was true from a macro perspective, she was about to find out that the attack was going to change her family's life as well.

Her husband was in the party rental business and was enjoying the fruits of the economy and the cultural norms of that time. After 9/11, everything changed. No one wanted to host parties—at least not in the immediate future. Business declined, and her husband lost his job. There they were—a stay-at-home mom and an unemployed dad wondering what was happening in our country and what was going to happen in their home.

As the days and months passed, they experienced something they had never experienced before. Over and over and over again, they saw God's faithfulness expressed through His people. Groceries were left at the doorstep, checks came in the mail, meals were provided, child care was provided—and the list goes on. For more than four months God showed up and met every need. They were blown away!

Prayer

God, thank you for the incredible gift you have given me of peace of mind and heart. I know that the peace you give me can never be found in the world. I will never be troubled or afraid because I know you keep me in perfect peace as long as I trust in you and keep my thoughts fixed on you (John 14:27, page 824, and Isaiah 26:3, page 535).

Resting in God's Promises

The psalm we're going to look at now is a majestic one. Psalm 89 (pages 454-455) was written by a wise man named Ethan, who lived during David's and Solomon's time. In it, he pleads with God in the face of national disaster. He remembers God's covenant with His people and expects help because of His faithfulness. Although a lot takes place in this psalm (much of it distressing), it begins and ends on the same note.

How is verse 52 related to verse 1?

That is precisely the advantage of a personal relationship with God! Even in the midst of distressing times, we can praise God forever. Do you remember from the last chapter why this is? (Hint: Elisha and his servant, who were surrounded by the enemy.)

As a child of God, we do not have to be overwhelmed by circumstances. They are only temporary but His love is eternal. His faithfulness, His unchanging love, and His unfailing promises deserve our continual praise.

Read Psalm 89:1-4 (pages 454-455).

What two promises does the writer make in verse 1?

1. *proclaim faith*

2. *love & kindness forever*

What two truths does he state about God in verse 2?

1.

2. *Jesus*

What promise did he remind God of in verses 3 and 4?

Read 2 Samuel 7:8-16 (page 240).

This passage is where God promises David a son (Solomon) who will build a temple for Him. This was a direct promise in relation to David's immediate family. However, God also prophetically promised that an heir of David would be on the throne of Israel forever.

Read Luke 1:31-33 (page 779).

How does Luke 1:31-33 fulfill the promise made in Psalm 89:4 and the 2 Samuel passage?

his lenage make him King like David

Resting in His Power

Read Psalm 89:5-14.

What specific attributes is the psalmist praising God for?

his majestic faithful justice

Verse 8 tells us no one is as powerful as God.

What does Psalm 62:11 (page 440) say?

What do the following New Testament verses say about God's power?

Matthew 19:26 (page 750)

every thing possible with God

Luke 1:37 (page 780)

"Nothing is impossible!" Nothing! Do you see what an incredible God we have? He is the Creator and owner of everything. Read the following verses and note what they say.

Psalm 50:10-11 (page 436)

he owns everything

Psalm 24:1 (page 423)

Hebrews 1:2-3 (page 920)

Gods Son

1 Corinthians 6:19-20 (page 873)

Psalm 89:12 mentions God creating Mt. Tabor and Mt. Hermon, which are prominent mountains. Mt. Tabor is a cone-shaped mountain covered with green grass and trees, located in Galilee. It has an elevation of more than 1800 feet. Mt. Hermon is a snow-capped mountain cluster northeast of the Sea of Galilee, with an elevation of more than 9000 feet. These beautiful mountains reveal some of the unlimited scope of God's creative power. He truly is worthy of praise.

In verses 13-14, what attributes of God are described?

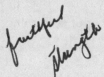

faithful
strength

Now read verses 15-16 and note the description of the people who follow Christ.

blessed   *hand in hand*

Do you see the connection between worship and walking in the light of God's presence? They go hand in hand. When you worship God, you are immersed in a sense of His presence. When you experience His presence, you can't help but worship.

Read verses 17 and 18.

These two verses sum up what the psalmist has said so far about God's power and faithfulness. And what a great summation, because what does verse 17 say pleases God?

powerful strength glory

God loves for us to allow Him to make us strong. How do each of these verses support how God is our strength?

2 Corinthians 12:9 (page 888)

salvation strength father, God

Exodus 15:2 (page 55)

my shield Helper

Psalm 28:7 (page 425)

Trusting Him for the Future

any —

Beginning with Psalm 89:19, the theme of this psalm switches to God's promises, with which the Bible is filled. Some of the promises we can access right now. They are designed to give us strength, courage, peace, joy—an ongoing list of blessings to enhance our lives on earth. Other promises are awaiting us in the future—yes, on earth and in heaven. The most incredible promise of all was God's promise of a Savior to save us from our sins and the wrath of God. Much of the last half of this psalm refers to this promise.

Read Psalm 89:19-29 (page 455).

One of the key reasons we can tell this passage refers to Christ is found in verse 26. Not once, in the Old Testament, does David, or anyone else, call God his Father when talking to Him in prayer. Jesus was the first to call God "Father," and He taught His followers to do the same. Read the following verses:

Matthew 5:16 (page 736)
Matthew 6:9 (page 737)
Romans 8:15 (page 862)

David, who wrote many of the psalms, was the second king of the Jewish nation. God told him that one of his descendants would be king forever. Old Testament prophets told more about this descendant who would come. They said He would be the Savior of the world as well as the King Eternal.

When Jesus Christ came as a baby, His earthly lineage through His mother, Mary, went back to David and further back to Abraham. He came as the Savior who God had promised the Jewish nation. However, since He came as a baby, the Jewish nation failed to recognize Him because they were expecting a king. Ultimately, they rejected Him.

God's promise to David was that Christ would be King of all the earth and rule forever. This promise has yet to be fulfilled. Verse 27 refers to *"my firstborn son."* We know this is a prophecy referring to Jesus, the firstborn and only Son of God, and not to David, who was the last-born son of Jesse. Verses 35-37 continue the prophecy with the promise that Jesus will establish a permanent Kingdom.

Read Psalm 89:30-37.

Even though God has to discipline and punish His people, what does it say He will never do?

No matter how badly we fail, God will never stop loving us, and He will never go back on His word. God promised that Jesus will establish a permanent Kingdom.

Read Psalm 89:38-45.

Ethan just finished recounting God's words. God promised that He would not break His covenant to His people and that one of David's ancestors would always be on the throne. Then in verses 38-45, Ethan complains that God had rejected the royal line and had broken His covenant. Have you ever complained to God just to see His faithfulness the next day?

Hundreds of years came between the last king's reign and the birth of Jesus Christ, who will be the final Davidic king. But Ethan did not know this and was voicing his frustrations to God. God wants us to come to Him when we are frustrated.

Read Psalm 89:46-51. This is a prayer of deliverance.

What emotions do you think Ethan is feeling as he asks God these questions?

Again, think of a time when you have felt those feelings. What questions did you ask God? How did God respond to them?

Trust

Look for phrases that give you a glimpse of Ethan's motivation for what he wrote. What do you think his motivation was?

In spite of Ethan's frustration and complaints, he finished his psalm with praise for the Lord forever. Like Ethan, even though we may not be able to see the big picture in the overall scheme of time, we need to acknowledge that God is God and is in control and is faithful to keep His promises.

Is there an area where you are frustrated with God's timing in your life? Take some time to write out your own psalm to God. Feel free to voice your frustrations and thoughts, but don't forget to praise Him for who you know He is.

Personal Reflection and Application

From this chapter,

I see…

I believe…

I will…

Prayer

O Lord, you are a shield around me; you are my glory, the one who holds my head high. I cry out to you and you answer me. I lie down and sleep and wake up in safety for you are watching over me (Psalm 3:3-5, page 415).

Thoughts, Notes, and Prayer Requests

_____

_____

_____

_____

_____

_____

_____

Christ—The Eternal Priest and King
Psalm 110

The tuberculosis hospital in Mafraq, Jordan, was in dire need. Their only vehicle had just been commandeered by the Jordanian army, leaving the staff stranded in the unforgiving desert, 50 miles from the nearest city, Amman. They had no way to get supplies or transport patients if the need arose.

Franklin Graham, a teenager at the time, had spent several summers in Jordan and always visited the hospital. He relayed the urgent need to his parents in a phone call. Did they know someone in London who could get a Land Rover by next Monday? He added, "And it has to be fully equipped for the desert." Ruth Graham promised to see what she could do.

Ruth shared the problem with Billy, who placed a call to a friend in London. Jean Wilson didn't bat an eye at the request. She went straight to the nearest Land Rover dealer, and after greeting him with abundant cheer, told him she needed a Land Rover, fully equipped for the desert, and she would pick it up Monday morning.

The salesman stared in disbelief. "But madam," he replied, "one does not simply ask for a Land Rover fully equipped for the desert and expect to pick it up on such short notice. One places one's order, and after a year, one picks—"

"I know, I know," Jean interrupted, "but I happen to need one by this coming Monday morning." They went back and forth a few more minutes, and finally Jean asked if he would please just check the warehouse to see if there happened to be a fully-equipped-for-the-desert Land Rover tucked away somewhere.

"Yes, madam," the salesman replied stiffly, and huffed off through the nearest door.

After some time he returned, a look of disbelief on his face. "Madam…" he stammered, "I, I do not understand…it was most unlikely, unthinkable…but I find we do happen to have a Land Rover in the warehouse, fully equipped for the desert." Sitting down behind his desk, he added, "And you may pick it up on Monday!"*

The Bible tells us that God knows our needs even before we ask Him (Matthew 6:8, page 737). It also tells us that He has promised to supply our needs (Philippians 4:19, page 901). Add that to the fact that His resources are unlimited. Is it any surprise that a Land Rover, fully equipped for the desert, was made available by Monday morning? The God we serve is a God for whom nothing is impossible, when our hearts are turned toward Him!

⪧

Prayer

How good it is to be near you, God! I have made you my shelter, and I will tell everyone about the wonderful things you do. O Lord, you are so good, so ready to forgive, so full of unfailing love for all who ask for your help (Psalm 73:28, page 446, and Psalm 86:5, page 453).

---

*Ruth Bell Graham, *Legacy of a Pack Rat* (Nashville, TN: Oliver-Nelson Books, 1989), pages 113-115.

The Mighty Priest and King

The psalm we're going to look at in this chapter is quoted 23 times in the New Testament—more than any other psalm. Seven of those times, it was Jesus who quoted it. No wonder Augustine spoke of this psalm as "brief in the number of words, but great in the weight of its thought." Martin Luther called it, "the true, high, main Psalm of our beloved Lord Jesus Christ." Does this make you eager to read it? It is only seven verses long, so let's read it all right now. It is Psalm 110 (page 465).

Okay now, be honest. After reading it, are you sitting there saying, *Huh?* Were you expecting something with a bit more "wow" factor after the opening buildup? Well, let's take a closer look and then re-evaluate.

First of all, did you notice that two high positions are referred to in this passage? Verse 2 talks about a king ruling his enemies and verse 4 mentions a priest. These two references are the key reasons that we know this psalm is referring to Jesus.

Just for some quick background, Israel was divided into 12 tribes. God decreed that all of Israel's priests were to be from the tribe of Levi. David was from the tribe of Judah, so he was not qualified to be a priest. Since this psalm refers to one person being both king and priest, we know it is not talking about David. Instead, it is a prediction of Christ Jesus. The fact that Jesus would one day be both King and Priest is confirmed in the New Testament. Read Matthew 22:41-45 (page 753).

Jesus is telling the Pharisees that David was inspired by the Holy Spirit when writing this psalm and that the psalm referred to Himself, Jesus—not to David.

Another interesting thing to notice about Psalm 110 is in the first verse. Did you notice it speaks of both God and Christ in the same sentence: *"The LORD said to my Lord"*?

If you remember from the first chapter, *LORD* translates *Yahweh*, God's personal name as the All-sufficient One, and *Lord* (*Adonai*) refers to the Lord, Master, or Ruler. Verse 1 can be read this way:

"Yahweh said to the Lord…" We can read it with this application: "God said to Christ, *'Sit in the place of honor at my right hand…'*" God, Yahweh, designated the position of honor for the Lord—Jesus Christ, the Messiah—at His own right hand, showing He is equal in position and authority with Himself. This is hard to comprehend, but of the three divine Persons in the Trinity—God the Father, God the Son, and God the Holy Spirit—we clearly see two of them in this first verse.

Read the following passages and note when Psalm 110:1 was fulfilled.

Hebrews 1:3 (page 920)

Hebrews 10:12-13 (page 925)

"Sit in the place of honor at my right hand" were the words God welcomed Jesus with when He returned to heaven at the close of His earthly ministry. Jesus spoke of His return to heaven after His resurrection in John 20:17 (page 828).

How did Jesus refer to His Father and God?

Jesus' death and resurrection is what made it possible for us to become joint heirs with Jesus in our heavenly Father's Kingdom. Somehow, those words of assurance from Jesus—*"my Father and your Father, to my God and your God"*—after His horrible suffering are precious.

Christ's Kingdom Is Established

When we studied Psalm 72 (chapter 2), we learned about the reign of Christ on the earth. Look again at Psalm 110:2-3. What does verse 2 say God will do to Christ's Kingdom?

When Christ returns the second time, His Kingdom will include the whole earth. And according to verse 3, how will people serve Him?

come willing

How often will your strength be renewed?

every day

His strength will be renewed just like "*the morning dew.*" It is wonderful to know that we are following someone who never grows weak or weary! His strength will never fail or falter. Isaiah 42:4a (page 549) reiterates this when it says, "*He will not falter or lose heart until justice prevails throughout the earth.*"

Our Great Priest Before God

In Genesis 14 (page 12) a somewhat mysterious King of Salem, who also was a priest of God Most High, is mentioned. His name was Melchizedek, and he was both a king and priest—which is what Jesus will be when He returns. There is a greater priesthood than the priesthood that comes through the line of Levi. Melchizedek's priesthood and kingship foreshadow the eternal priesthood and reign of Christ as King.

But what is the significance of Christ being our High Priest? Read the following verses to find out.

Hebrews 7:23-28 (pages 923-924)

1 Timothy 2:5-6 (page 910)

Hebrews 7:25b and 1 Timothy 2:5 describe Jesus in the same way. What is it?

Before Jesus' death, a human priest was the mediator for Israel. All of humanity is fallible, not to mention mortal. But Jesus is both perfect and eternal. He is the ongoing Mediator between people and God. I love the way Romans 8:34 paraphrases this in *The Message*:

> *The One who died for us—who was raised to life for us!—*
> *is in the presence of God at this very moment sticking up for us.*

Isn't that a wonderful picture? Jesus is sticking up for *us*! How should that impact the way you live?

Victory over Enemies *Meth Kine*

As you've probably noticed, this psalm has a military flavor, with references to enemies, war, and kingdoms. Verse 5 begins to describe the complete victory over the enemy that is coming.

> What are some personal enemies you long to gain victory over? Think in terms of attitudes, habits, desires—anything that interferes with your ability to live 100 percent for Christ.

> Why don't you take some time right now and hold out to God what you've written down? Ask Him to help you defeat every enemy that stands between you and the life He wants you to experience. As you pray, take time to listen. Jot down any thoughts God brings to your mind.

salt

God does not intend for us to fight these battles alone. He has filled the Bible with instructions that will lead us to victory. Look up the following verses to see what instructions are given in each one.

1 Timothy 6:11 (page 913)

What does this verse tell us to pursue?

faith
endurance
love

Do you remember that wonderful verse, Psalm 23:6, about God pursuing us? Now it's our turn to reciprocate. Don't just meander in the general direction of a godly life, but pursue it with all your heart and mind!

2 Corinthians 10:4 (page 887)

This is such an important verse! We can so easily fall prey to human reasoning that is, when closely examined, in complete opposition to God's Word! And false arguments too!

What are some examples of misleading false arguments or reasoning?

Obey Christ
& prayer

How does it tell us to defend ourselves against these things?

What are some of God's mighty weapons?

angels   breastplate   faith

The mightiest weapon of all is truth, and we find truth in the Bible. The more familiar we are with what God's Word says, the less likely we'll be to fall prey to human reasoning and false arguments.

1 John 5:4 (page 943)

Who does it say defeats the evil world?

our faith

Every child of God! *Every single one*! We are assured of achieving victory through what means?

faith

Faith in God! By faith, we have victory over the world by understanding that the things that we see on earth are temporary and will perish. It is only the things done for Christ and His Kingdom that will last. We will receive ultimate victory because Christ is our King, and He has already conquered the enemy through His death on the cross and resurrection. Read the following verses:

Ephesians 2:1-6 (page 895) *headed for punishment*

Now read Hebrews 11:29-34 (page 927).

List some of the impossible circumstances that faith gained victory over.

Just because these people overcame difficult circumstances through their faith does not mean that their lives were easy or pain-free. *"They shut the mouths of lions, quenched the flames of fire, and escaped death by the edge of the sword."* That doesn't sound easy to me. No matter how hard the trial may have been, though, God led them through these difficult situations, helping them remember that the things of this world are just temporary and that He has already won the war.

Are you feeling positively victorious right now—capable of defeating every enemy you are facing? You should be, because what does the very last phrase of Psalm 110:7 say?

Wow! Amen!

—————— *Personal Reflection and Application* ——————

From this chapter,

I see...

I believe...

I will...

————————————— ✎ —————————————

Prayer

    Lord, I will never stop praising you; I will declare your glory all day long. Your unfailing love, O Lord, is as vast as the heavens; your faithfulness reaches beyond the clouds. I find shelter in the shadow of your wings (Psalm 71:8, page 445, and Psalm 36:5,7b, page 429).

—————— *Thoughts, Notes, and Prayer Requests* ——————

_____

_____

_____

_____

_____

_____

_____

_____

11

Christ—The Cornerstone
Psalm 118

The sound of a doorbell is innocuous—except when it acts as an alarm clock you didn't set. The jarring, unsettling sound jerked me from bed just after dawn. Hurrying into some clothes, I sensed our world was about to change. Five policemen stood at our door with a search warrant in hand. Stunned, feeling like I'd awakened in the middle of the Twilight Zone, I watched them invade our home, going through every cupboard and drawer of every room, searching for evidence that wasn't there and never had been.

We later learned simultaneous raids had been conducted by state police on the homes of several other business owners, investigating possible illegal collusion among them. Each was charged with the felony offense of racketeering. Just that easily we were thrust into a legal nightmare of gargantuan proportions that stretched out nearly three years. Worse than the sickening outflow of money to protect ourselves was the attack on our reputation, which even the officer behind the investigation admitted was stellar.

In the beginning, sleep was impossible as worst-case scenarios whirled through my mind. Even my prayer time became haunted—the very act of giving voice to our circumstances in prayer served to pull my attention more toward the battle we faced rather than God. One morning, my trembling fingers stumbled on Psalm 86. *"Bend down, O LORD, and hear my prayer; answer me, for I need your help…hear my urgent cry…You alone are God…insolent people rise up against me…you are a God of compassion and mercy…"* (page 453).

Every word was precisely applicable, and I devoured them as if they were my last chance for survival. That psalm proved to be my turning point. I memorized every word of it, repeating it all day long. The minute a fear thought entered my mind, I eradicated it with a portion of Psalm 86. The more permeated my mind became with the memorized words, the stronger and more confident I grew—willing to trust God with any outcome He chose to allow.

The end result of the ordeal was a stunning victory for the buisness owners. For me, however, the most stunning victory had come long before, when I began to saturate my soul with the truth I found in Psalm 86. That was the day I began to experience the power of God's Word to render every enemy defenseless.

❦

Prayer

Lord, thank you for the power of your Word—that when I hide it in my heart, it will keep me from sin. Don't let me lose sight of your words, but let them penetrate deep into my heart so they can bring life to me (Psalm 119:11, page 468, and Proverbs 4:21-22, page 483).

A Celebration of Praise

Psalm 118 is a processional psalm of celebration in which God is honored and praised. This song was used in Temple worship and traditionally was sung along with other psalms as part of the Passover observance.

The first four verses of Psalm 118 (page 467) are a call to worship. The leader gave the call, and the people answered with a refrain. Let's picture the scene. The people are gathered together to worship God. The priests in their ceremonial robes are at the front of the people ready to blow their trumpets and lead the procession. When everything is ready, the worship leader shouts out the first line of praise: *"Give thanks to the LORD, for he is good!"*

The huge crowd shouts back in response, *"His faithful love endures forever!"*

As you read these verses, imagine the worship leader calling out each line and the crowd shouting back their enthusiastic response. Imagine how the excitement would build each time the people shouted back the refrain, *"His faithful love endures forever!"*

Worship and praise are such an essential aspect of our relationship with God. Praise is a powerful protection against all the challenging circumstances of life, because it keeps our focus on God and not on the circumstances.

Read the following verses. What do they all have in common?

Psalm 35:28 (page 429)

Psalm 71:14 (page 445)

Psalm 104:33 (page 461)

Psalm 145:1 (page 478)

Praise is as much an attitude as it is an action—being in a constant state of awareness of God's goodness and having an abiding sense of gratitude for His love. What can you do to develop this attitude?

It goes back to our very first chapter, doesn't it? Meditating on God's Word, memorizing it, and incorporating it fully into our minds so that it influences our thought processes and reactions to things that go on throughout the day.

> *God's loving mercy never ceases.*
> *Neither should our praise.*

The One We Can Rest On

The next section of verses is hugely comforting, no matter what circumstance we're facing. Read Psalm 118:5-9 (pages 467-468).

What did God do when the psalmist cried out to Him?

How do you think God set him free?

There are many times when our cries for help are not answered in the way we want. But God has promised, even in the heartbreak and disappointment of those times, that He will free us of the attitudes that make those circumstances unbearable. He can counter our grief with His inexpressible love. He can replace our fear and dread with trust. He can exchange our worry for peace. Think of a time when you or someone you know has experienced this shift in attitude.

What were the circumstances and how did God respond?

If God is for us, then who can be against us? This truth is referenced throughout the Bible. For example, read Romans 8:31 (page 863) and Hebrews 13:5-6 (page 928).

God has surrounded us with incredible truth about His character that shows we can have complete trust in Him because no one and nothing is more powerful or capable than God!

One of the best ways to build your trust is through a prayer journal. Start recording your prayers in a notebook and keep track of how you see God working in each circumstance. Or you may want to blog or share your prayer journal with a trusted friend. You will be amazed at what you record over time.

With the passage of time, even the most spectacular answers to prayer are forgotten. Things you think you'll remember fade into oblivion as new occurrences take their place. God understands this human tendency. That's why He taught the Israelites to always keep a record. Read Joshua 4:1-7 (pages 169-170).

The memorial was to remind them, and future generations, of the time God backed up the water of the Jordan River so the people could cross on dry ground. I find this fascinating because I cannot imagine that I would ever forget something as dramatic as a river parting so

I could cross on dry ground. Now, pretend that you were one of the Israelites crossing over the Jordan River on dry ground.

What circumstances could happen so that you might forget this particular experience?

Even remarkable events such as this one eventually fade into the background. Or even if we don't forget, we never think about them until something pricks our memory. That memorial God had them build became an ongoing reminder of His miraculous intervention on their behalf. Often in the Old Testament, when something significant happened, God told the Israelites to build a memorial.

And just as their piles of stones reminded them of God's interventions, a prayer journal does the same for us today. It becomes tangible proof that God, who once rolled back the Jordan River for the Israelites, is doing remarkable things for us! Our spiritual journal can be a constant reminder to us, and our future generations, of what God has done.

Facing Disappointment Victoriously

Now, back to Psalm 118. Read verses 8 and 9 (page 468).

Think of a time when you have been let down by someone you trusted.

We've all experienced this. It's part of being human—we are fallible. Sometimes, even with the best of intentions, trusted people fail us. God, however, will not fail us. He is the only sure refuge in this life.

The next four verses of Psalm 118 describe a time when the psalmist was inundated with trouble. Read verses 10-14.

Wow! Have you ever had days like that? Maybe weeks or months when it seemed like troubles swarmed around you like bees? How have you handled those times?

How did the psalmist respond to his circumstances?

What exactly do you think he meant when he said, *"I destroyed them all with the authority of the LORD"*?

In spite of the litany of problems he faced in these verses, do you sense any distress in his words?

He sounds pretty matter of fact as he lists them—no emotion or angst is apparent. But there *is* emotion in his response. The words ring with victory. He obviously had learned that if you focus on the circumstances, the impossibilities they present grow bigger and fiercer until you're paralyzed, unable to move in any direction that is productive or healthy. However, if you maintain a sharp, clear focus on God—who has authority over all creation—it will keep the circumstances in perspective; it will break them down to a size you can manage.

Can you think of a time when God absolutely stunned you with the way He destroyed a terrifying circumstance you were facing? Please explain.

How does the psalmist describe God in verse 14?

What kind of attitude usually accompanies singing?

He is saying that God not only strengthens him, but God also lifts his attitude even in the midst of attacks. And, according to the very last phrase of verse 14, what is the result of that combination?

Amazing, isn't it? Are you overwhelmed with gratitude for how willing God is to help? Why don't you take a moment and write down some of your thoughts.

The Righteous Enter the Gates

We've gotten a bit distracted from the celebration taking place at the Temple, but verses 19-21 bring us back. Picture again the people who have been singing as they walked toward the Temple. And now, as they approach the gates, it is likely they began to sing verse 19. Imagine them singing in loud and eager anticipation: *"Open for me the gates where the righteous enter, and I will go in and thank the LORD."*

The gatekeeper's answer to them would have been verse 20: *"These gates lead to the presence of the LORD, and the godly enter there."*

As we've already discussed, it is our acceptance of Jesus' death for our sins that makes us righteous before God. No substitute will work. It doesn't matter how hard we work to live a good life, how much we strive for peace and justice, or how committed we are to our church. The only way we can be righteous in God's eyes is by acknowledging Jesus as our Savior.

If you have any hesitation in answering yes to one of the following questions, read the verse next to it.

- Do you believe God loves you? Romans 5:8 (page 860)

- Do you believe Jesus is God's Son? 1 John 4:9 (page 943)

- Do you believe Jesus Christ died for you? Galatians 2:20 (page 891)

- Have you received Jesus Christ as your Savior? John 1:12 (page 809)

- Does Christ live in you? Ephesians 3:17 (page 896)

If you answered no to any of these questions, just tell God right now that, even though you still have lots of questions, you are willing to put your faith in Him. He will answer your questions as your relationship grows, but the first step is to give Him access to your life. If you like, turn to "Know God" on pages 177–179 and pray the prayer written there.

Taking Joy in Christ, Our Cornerstone

A cornerstone is the first stone set in the foundation of a building. It is the most important stone because all the others in the foundation are laid in reference to it. In fact, the cornerstone determines the position of the entire building.

Jesus is referred to as the Cornerstone in both the Old and New Testaments, and Psalm 118 includes one of those references.

Psalm 118:22-23 is the part of the psalm that is messianic. The Cornerstone it talks about refers to Christ. Read the following verses:

Mark 12:10-11 (page 773)
Acts 4:11 (page 833)
1 Peter 2:6-7 (page 935)

One of the most wonderful verses about Christ being the Cornerstone is Isaiah 28:16 (page 537). How is the cornerstone described?

The last two sentences are powerful, aren't they? *"It is a precious cornerstone that is safe to build on. Whoever believes need never be shaken."* What wonderful reassurance for us!

Interestingly, Christ is often referred to in Scripture as a foundation, rock, or stone. Note what the following verses say:

1 Corinthians 3:11 (page 871)

Ephesians 2:20 (page 896)

1 Peter 2:4-7 (page 935)

Romans 9:32-33 (page 864)

The last passage described Jesus as a different kind of stone. What is it?

For each of us, Christ is either our Cornerstone or a stone to stumble over. If we believe in Him, He is our Cornerstone. If we don't, He is a stone we stumble over. What is Jesus to you?

Psalm 118:24 is a verse we should tape to our bathroom mirror so we see it first thing in the morning. We should tape it to the dash of our car as a reminder while we're driving. We should make it visible in all the places where we are more likely to complain than be thankful. What does it say?

Did you notice the phrasing? *"We* will *rejoice."* Rejoicing is not only a reaction to our circumstances. It is a *determination of our will.* Whatever the day brings, we will rejoice—if not over the circumstance, over God who walks through the circumstance with us, infusing us with His strength.

The last four verses of the psalm are words of pure praise as the sacrifice is laid on the altar. Read verses 26-29.

The first sentence of verse 26, *"Bless the one who comes in the name of the LORD,"* is repeated six times in the New Testament in reference to Jesus' mission on earth. Can you hear the joy in their voices as they praise God? The very last words of the psalm are the same words it began with: *"Give thanks to the LORD, for he is good! His faithful love endures forever."*

It has been a pleasure exploring some of the psalms with you! Hopefully it has whetted your appetite to explore the book of Psalms more fully, because we barely scratched the surface. May you always *"delight in the law of the LORD, meditating on it day and night"* (Psalm 1:2, page 415).

———————— *Personal Reflection and Application* ————————

From this chapter,

I see…

I believe…

I will…

Prayer

Your unfailing love, O Lord, is as vast as the heavens; your faithfulness reaches beyond the clouds. Because of Jesus I will offer a continual sacrifice of praise to you, proclaiming my allegiance to your name because *your faithful love endures forever* (Psalm 36:5, page 429; Hebrews 13:15, page 929; and Psalm 118:1, page 467).

Thoughts, Notes, and Prayer Requests

Journal Pages

Know God

It does not matter what has happened in your past. No matter what you've done, no matter how you've lived your life,

God is personally interested in you right now.
He cares about you.

God understands your frustration, your loneliness, your heart-aches. He wants each of us to come to Him, to know Him personally.

God is so rich in mercy, and he loved us so much, that even
though we were dead because of our sins, he gave us
life when he raised Christ from the dead.
(It is only by God's grace that you have been saved!)

—*Ephesians 2:4-5 (page 895)*

God loves you.

He created you in His image. His desire is to be in relationship with you. He wants you to belong to Him.

Sadly, our sin gets in the way. It separates us from God, and without Him we are dead in our spirits. There is nothing we can do to close that gap. There is nothing we can do to give ourselves life. No matter how well we may behave.

But God loves us so much He made a way to eliminate that gap and give us new life, His kind of life—to restore the relationship. His love for us is so great, so tremendous, that He sent Jesus Christ, His only Son, to earth to live, and then die—filling the gap and taking the punishment we deserve for refusing God's ways.

God made Christ, who never sinned,
to be the offering for our sin, so that we could
be made right with God through Christ.

—*2 Corinthians 5:21 (page 884)*

Jesus Christ, God's Son, not only died to pay the penalty for your sin, but He conquered death when He rose from the grave. He is ready to share His life with you.

Christ reconciles us to God. Jesus is alive today. He will give you a new beginning and a newly created life when you surrender control of your life to Him.

Anyone who belongs to Christ has become a new
person. The old life is gone; a new life has begun!

—*2 Corinthians 5:17 (page 884)*

How do you begin this new life? You need to realize

...the necessity of repenting from sin and turning to
God, and of having faith in our Lord Jesus.

—*Acts 20:21 (page 849)*

Agree with God about your sins and believe that Jesus came to save you, that He is your Savior and Lord. Ask Him to lead your life.

God loved the world so much that he gave his
one and only Son, so that everyone who believes in him
will not perish but have eternal life.
God sent his Son into the world not to judge the
world, but to save the world through him.

—*John 3:16-17 (page 811)*

Pray something like this:

Jesus, I do believe you are the Son of God and that you died on the cross to pay the penalty for my sin. Forgive me. I turn away from my sin and choose to live a life that pleases you. Enter my life as my Savior and Lord.

I want to follow you and make you the leader of my life.

Thank you for your gift of eternal life and for the Holy Spirit, who has now come to live in me. I ask this in your name. Amen.

God puts His Spirit inside you, who enables you to live a life pleasing to Him. He gives you new life that will never die, that will last forever—eternally.

When you surrender your life to Jesus Christ, you are making the most important decision of your life. Stonecroft would like to offer you a free download of *A New Beginning*, a short Bible study that will help you as you begin your new life in Christ. Go to **stonecroft.org/ newbeginning**.

If you'd like to talk with someone right now about this prayer, call **1.888.NEED.HIM.**

Who Is Stonecroft?

Every day Stonecroft communicates the Gospel in meaningful ways. Whether side by side with a neighbor or new friend, or through a speaker sharing her transformational story, the Gospel of Jesus Christ goes forward. Through a variety of outreach activities and small group Bible studies specifically designed for those not familiar with God, and with online and print resources focused on evangelism, Stonecroft proclaims the Gospel of Jesus Christ to women where they are, as they are.

For more than 75 years, always with a foundation of prayer in reliance on God, Stonecroft volunteers have found ways to introduce women to Jesus Christ and train them to share His Good News with others.

Stonecroft understands and appreciates the influence of one woman's life. When you reach her, you touch everyone she knows—her family, friends, neighbors, and co-workers. The real Truth of the Gospel brings real redemption into real lives.

Our life-changing, faith-building community resources include:

- ***Stonecroft Bible and Book Studies***—both topical and chapter-by-chapter studies. We designed Stonecroft studies for those in small groups—those who know Christ and those who do not yet know Him—to simply yet profoundly discover God's Word together.

- **Stonecroft Prays!**—calls small groups of women together to pray for God to show them avenues to reach women in their community with the Gospel.

- **Outreach Events**—set the stage for women to hear and share the Gospel with their communities. Whether in a large venue, workshop, or small group setting, Stonecroft women find ways to share the love of Christ.

- **Stonecroft Military**—a specialized effort to honor women connected to the U.S. military and share with them the Gospel while showing them the love of Christ.

- **Small Group Studies for Christians**—these resources reveal God's heart for those who do not yet know Him. The Aware Series includes *Aware, Belong,* and *Call.*

- **Stonecroft Life Publications**—clearly explain the Gospel through stories of people whose lives have been transformed by Jesus Christ.

- **Stonecroft.org**—offers fresh content daily to equip and encourage you.

Dedicated and enthusiastic Stonecroft staff serve you via Divisional Field Directors stationed across the United States, and a Home Office team who support tens of thousands of dedicated volunteers worldwide.

Your life matters. Join us today to impact your communities with the Gospel of Jesus Christ. Become involved with Stonecroft.

STONECROFT

Get started: connections@stonecroft.org 800.525.8627	Support Stonecroft: stonecroft.org/donate	Order resources: stonecroft.org/store 888.819.5218

Books for Further Study

Keller, Phillip W. *A Shepherd Looks at Psalm 23*. Grand Rapids, MI: Zondervan, 2007.

Lewis, C.S. *Reflections on the Psalms*. Orlando, FL: Harcourt, Inc., 1958.

Longman, Tremper III. *How to Read the Psalms*. Downers Grove, IL: InterVarsity Press, 1988.

Pfeiffer, Charles F., and Everett F. Harrison, *The Wycliffe Bible Commentary*. Chicago, IL: Moody Press, 1963.

Spurgeon, Charles. *The Treasury of David. Volumes I-VI*. Grand Rapids, MI: Zondervan, 1950.

Travers, Michael E. *Encountering God in the Psalms*. Grand Rapids, MI: Kregel Publications, 2003.

Stonecroft Resources

Stonecroft Bible Studies make the Word of God accessible to everyone. These studies allow small groups to discover the adventure of a personal relationship with God and introduce others to God's unlimited love, grace, forgiveness, and power. To learn more, visit **stonecroft.org/biblestudies**.

Who Is Jesus? (6 chapters)
He was a rebel against the status quo. The religious community viewed Him as a threat. The helpless and outcast considered Him a friend. Explore the life and teachings of Jesus—this rebel with a cause who challenges us today to a life of radical faith.

What Is God Like? (6 chapters)
What is God like? Is He just a higher power? Has He created us and left us on our own? Where is He when things don't make sense? Discover what the Bible tells us about God and how we can know Him in a life-transforming way.

Who Is the Holy Spirit? (6 chapters)
Are you living up to the full life that God wants for you? Learn about the Holy Spirit, our Helper and power source for everyday living, who works in perfect harmony with God the Father and Jesus the Son.

Connecting with God (8 chapters)
Prayer is our heart-to-heart communication with our heavenly Father. This study examines the purpose, power, and elements of prayer, sharing biblical principles for effective prayer.

Today I Pray

When we bow before God on behalf of someone who doesn't yet know of His saving work, of His great love in sending His Son Jesus, of His mercy and goodness, we enter into a work that has eternal impact. Stonecroft designed *Today I Pray* as a 30-day intercessory prayer commitment that you may use to focus your prayers on behalf of a specific person, or to pray for many—because your prayers are powerful and important!

Prayer Worth Repeating (15 devotions)

There is no place where your prayers to the one and only God cannot penetrate, no circumstance prayers cannot impact. As the mother of adult children, your greatest influence into their lives is through prayer. *Prayer Worth Repeating* is a devotional prayer guide designed to focus your prayers and encourage you to trust God more deeply as He works in the lives of your adult children.

Pray & Play Devotional (12 devotions)

It's playgroup with a purpose! Plus Mom tips. For details on starting a Pray & Play group, visit **stonecroft.org/prayandplay** or call **800.525.8627**.

Prayer Journal

A practical resource to strengthen your prayer life, this booklet includes an introductory section about the importance of prayer, the basic elements of prayer, and a clear Gospel presentation, as well as 40 pages of journaling your prayer requests and God's answers.

Prayer—Talking with God

This booklet provides insight and biblical principles to help you establish a stronger, more effective prayer life.

Aware (5 lessons)
Making Jesus known every day starts when we are *Aware* of those around us. This dynamic Stonecroft Small Group Bible Study about "Always Watching and Responding with Encouragement" equips and engages people in the initial steps to the joys of evangelism.

Belong (6 lessons)
For many in today's culture, the desire to belong is often part of their journey to believe. *Belong* explores how we can follow in Jesus' footsteps—and walk with others on their journey to belong.

Call (7 lessons)
Every day we meet people without Christ. That is God's intention.

He wants His people to initiate and build friendships. He wants us together. *Call* helps us take a closer look at how God makes Himself known through our relationships with those around us.

Discover together God's clear calling for you and those near to you.

These and many more Stonecroft resources are available to you.

Order today to impact your communities with the
Gospel of Jesus Christ.
Simply visit **stonecroft.org/store** to get started.

If you have been encouraged and brought closer to God by this study, please consider giving a gift to Stonecroft so that others can experience life change as well. You can find information about giving online at **stonecroft.org.** (Click on the "Donate" tab.)

If you'd like to give via telephone, please contact us at **800.525.8627.** Or you can mail your gift to

Stonecroft
PO Box 9609
Kansas City, MO 64134-0609

STONECROFT

PO Box 9609, Kansas City, MO 64134-0609
Telephone: 816.763.7800 | 800.525.8627
E-mail: connections@stonecroft.org | stonecroft.org

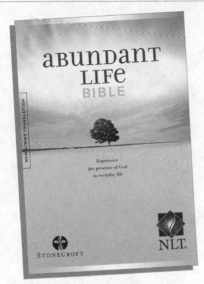

Abundant Life Bible
New Living Translation
Holy Bible

Experience the presence of God
in everyday life

Stonecroft is pleased to partner with Tyndale to offer the New Living Translation Holy Bible as the companion for our newly released Stonecroft Bible Studies.

The New Living Translation translators set out to render the message of the original Scripture language texts into clear, contemporary English. In this *translation*, scholars kept the concerns of both formal-equivalence and dynamic-equivalence in mind. Their goal was a Bible that is faithful to the ancient texts and eminently readable. The result is a translation that is both accurate and powerful.

TRUTH MADE CLEAR

Features of the Abundant Life Bible

- Features are easy-to-use and written for people who don't yet know Jesus Christ personally.

- Unequaled clarity and accuracy

- Dictionary included

- Concordance included

- Old Testament included

- Introductory notes on important abundant life topics such as:
  Gospel presentation   Practical guidance
  Joy   Life's tough issues
  Peace   Prayer

- Insights from a relationship with Jesus Christ.

- Ideal Scripture text for those not familiar with the Bible!

 Tyndale House Publishers

To order: stonecroft.org/store
800.525.8627

STONECROFT
stonecroft.org/SBS